LIVE LONGER THROUGH LAUGHTER

LIVE LONGER THROUGH LAUGHTER

JOEY ADAMS

Foreword by Norman Cousins

How to use a joke to save your health, your mind, your marriage, your election, your party, your speech, your business, or your friends

STEIN AND DAY/*Publishers*/New York

First published in 1984

Designed by Louis A. Ditizio
Printed in the United States of America
STEIN AND DAY/*Publishers*
Scarborough House
Briarcliff Manor, N.Y. 10510

Library of Congress Cataloging in Publication Data

Adams, Joey, 1911-
Live longer through laughter.

1. American wit and humor. I. Title.
PN6162.A336 1984 818′.5402 83-40361
ISBN 0-8128-2955-7

Contents

Foreword by Norman Cousins 7

Part I

1. Laughter Is a Cure-All 13
2. A Handbook of Humor for Politicians 17
3. How to Take a Joke—No Matter Whose It Is 27
4. The Roast of the Town—Laugh Prescriptives 43
5. A Dais in the Life of Everyone 63
6. A First-Aid Kit of Humor 73
7. Adam's Rib 79
8. Special Occasion Pick-Me-Ups 83

Part II

The Emergency Gag File—Yours for Adoption 91

Foreword

Some of the comments about a book I wrote under the title *Anatomy of an Illness* made it appear that I had laughed my way out of a serious health condition. Careful readers of the book, however, knew that I was emphasizing the importance of the full range of positive emotions as a vital factor in an effective partnership between physician and patient.

Laughter—along with hope, faith, love, will to live, creativity—can be regarded as an important resource in any strategy of recovery or, indeed, in prompting good health. Some medical researchers, like Dr. William F. Fry, Jr., of Stanford University, have written about the ability of laughter to enhance respiration and thus promote proper oxygenation of the blood. Other researchers have speculated that laughter can stimulate the production of endorphins and encephalins in the brain, substances with morphinelike molecules that provide the body with its own pain suppressors. The theory has also been advanced that laughter may stimulate the thymus gland, thus carrying out a useful role in the body's immunological functions.

Much more research needs to be carried out along these lines, of course. Meanwhile, one fact is clear. Few things are more important in treating disease than relieving the patient of the panic that generally accompanies a serious condition. For panic is a disease in itself, producing constriction of the blood vessels and disrupting the normal functioning of the immune system. Laughter, along with other positive emotions, serves an important purpose by acting as a panic-blocker. The role of blocking agents in the treatment of disease is well recognized. There are calcium-blockers and beta-blockers for certain categories of heart disease. Analgesics are blockers, too. Laughter becomes an important blocker against the ravages of runaway fears and helps to protect the body against the chain reaction of disease and panic.

I have the highest regard for the humorist in our society. The ability to make people laugh is not just a talent but a public asset. For almost half a century, Joey Adams has used humor seriously. That is, behind all his outrageously funny stories is a serious purpose. He knows that the sound of laughter is one of the healthiest sounds in the world. He realizes that laughter is a solvent, not just for pain but for all the ill feelings, animosities, and bad tempers that tend to disfigure our individual and collective existence. This book is his way of sharing with people his gift for recognizing the incongruities of life. In it Adams enables his readers to experience one of the prime elements of human uniqueness—the ability to enjoy wit and harmless folly. This is not Joey Adams's first book, but it is the most comprehensive he has yet done. In the new book we find his favorite stories, his way of nourishing the spirit of his fellow human beings.

During my own illness, I relished and was gratified by his knack for bringing together the vital materials of mirth. I remember one of Dr. Hitzig's prescription slips. At the bottom he wrote, "Take a Joey Adams story before and after medication."

I commend this prescription not just to those who have to take pills but to everyone who wants to avoid doing so.

Norman Cousins

LIVE LONGER THROUGH LAUGHTER

PART I

1
Laughter is a Cure-All

Laugh and the world laughs with you; cry and it means you can't take it—or worse, you can't dish it out. Jokes are the strongest weapons you can use and laughter is the greatest defense.

Laughter is a joy, and a dose of joy is a physical as well as a spiritual cure. MARTIN LUTHER KING, JR., always encouraged me to throw jokes instead of stones: "Laughter is love," he said, "and it's a great way to handle your enemies: 'Love the Hell out of them.'"

RONALD REAGAN throws those one-liners better than any stand-up comic: "When you're laughing," says R. R., "you're not worrying." The President proved his point when he was shot. The first thing he said after his operation was, "I'm sorry, Nancy, I forgot to duck." Everyone laughed and a lot of the tension was over.

MILTON BERLE opened and closed in a show called *Goodnight Grandpa*. After the reviews, it was *Goodbye Grandpa*, but not goodbye Berle. Milton beat everybody to the laughs. Although he had roasted many, he was now able to roast himself as well: "They gave the author a 21-gun salute—unfortunately they missed. . . . What can you expect? We opened under great difficulties—the curtain was up. . . . It wasn't easy doing a show in that theater," he explained. "The seats faced the stage."

It's Milton who got the last laugh and who was able to laugh himself well. That's the idea of this book—to prepare you for battle, to arm you with jokes, gags, stories, and answers in case you run into a heckler, a dais full of murderers, or an opponent with a scalpel. If the butcher, the baker, or the plumber is trying to beat you to the punch line, or an audience is looking to you for laughs, you will be ready.

BOB HOPE is always prepared if he's having dinner with friends or playing golf with the President. He has jokes ready for any emergency. Bob was toastmaster at a dinner for some astronauts, and one of them had the nerve to make a funny. Bob cracked, "If there's one thing I can't stand it's a smart astronaut."

Bob's writers work overtime when he's golfing with the President: "I know your handicap," he said to REAGAN, "it's the Congress," and the President laughed. Bob said to JIMMY CARTER, "I don't know why everybody is picking on you—you haven't done anything." Carter howled. Hope told GERALD FORD on the fourth hole, "You should be sent to Vietnam with a number three wood." Ford screamed.

Bob gives them a chance to return the laughs. He told RICHARD NIXON, "I wear ARNOLD PALMER shorts, Arnold Palmer shoes. I use Arnold Palmer clubs, and I play like BETSY PALMER."

PHYLLIS DILLER gets her biggest laughs by laughing at herself. I introduced Phyllis on my radio show as "the lady with a thousand gags." Phyllis interrupted, "A thousand and two—you forgot my face and figure."

Phyllis wants those laughs coming, no matter who the target may be—preferably herself: "I go to a beauty parlor that has a recovery room," she says. Phyllis preaches, "Marry a man your own age. As your beauty fades, so will his eyesight."

Phyllis wants those laughs: "The role of women is really changing. There's a little old lady lives next door to me who spends all her time reading *The Joy of Sex* and knitting a whip." Says our Phyllis, "I'm writing a book entitled 'Sex is the most fun you can have without laughing.'"

Age is a matter of mind. If you don't mind, it doesn't matter. GEORGE BURNS keeps himself well and young by laughing at age. "If your're old enough to know better, you're too old to do it." Or "I have a prune juice martini fix every meal." Or "old age is when you don't have to own antiques to sit down on something that's over eighty years old."

BOB HOPE, on reaching eighty, reached for his age lines: "I must be getting old—my sex drive has turned into a putt." Bob told me, "For excitement on Saturday night in North Hollywood, GEORGE BURNS, LAWRENCE WELK, VINCENT MINNELLI, and I sit around and watch to see whose leg falls asleep faster. Then we try to contact the living."

Laughter can save your marriage. MICHAEL YORK told me, "My wife and I love to laugh. We work hard at laughter. We play charades, do riddles, surprise each other with new jokes and gags. Laughing relieves an enzyme and makes for health."

When CINDY and I were married, I had the marriage vows changed. She promised to "love, laugh and applaud." Well, two out of three is not bad. Laughs bring love, and my home is filled with love. The walls of my home are filled with love, the furniture, the bed—well, not the bed so much. But, as Cindy says, my lovemaking *is* laughable. I'll take my laughs any way I can get them.

There are so many headaches in the world today that if MOSES came down from Mount Sinai now, the tablets he would carry would be Anacin. That's why God gave us a sense of humor—to turn tragedy into joy. And the way to do it is with laughter.

NORMAN COUSINS was ready to give up on life when he found the prescription called laughter. He got some Groucho Marx pictures, Laurel and Hardy pictures, and collected all the gags, jokes, and funny stories he could find. Before he could say, "A funny thing happened on the way to St. Peter," he was well and happy and ready to share the formula with everybody: "Laugh yourself well."

That's the idea of this book. Don't keep the faith, spread it around with laughter.

2
A Handbook of Humor for Politicians

Humor has been winning and losing votes for politicos ever since GEORGE WASHINGTON. I don't know what sort of a knee-slapper George was, but I know he was the only chief of state who didn't blame the previous administration for all his troubles.

A long time ago RICHARD NIXON lost an election because of those posters that read, "Would you buy a used car from this man?"

Several elections before, THOMAS E. DEWEY blew it when he was sliced with, "He looks like the groom on top of the wedding cake."

The greatest weapon a politician can use is laughter, whether he's attacking or defending.

No one used gags more skillfully than JOHN F. KENNEDY: "If Nixon runs unopposed he'll lose." Kennedy used his scalpel on everyone: "I like the straightforward way SENATOR MCCARTHY dodges all those issues." Or "BARRY GOLDWATER says he's standing on his record—that's so nobody can see it."

In Kennedy's case, humor was an integral part of his inspiration. His humor helped establish a national mood, and it got him out of a lot of trouble.

When J.F.K. became President of the United States, one of his first appointments was BOBBY KENNEDY, his brother, as Attorney General. The uproar was tremendous. There were shouts of nepotism. "He's only a kid, just out of law school." It was a tough spot for the new President.

I saw the President before he held his press conference and suggested the line that laughed him out of it. One reporter started, "How could you appoint a young boy, and your brother, just out of law school, as the Attorney General of the most powerful country in the world?" The Prez smiled, "Well, he's my kid brother, and I wanted to give him some experience before he opened his own law office." Everybody howled and the problem was over. J.F.K. had laughed himself out of trouble.

Another time he was accused of having his father buy him the Presidency. He solved this one with another laugh. At a White House correspondents' dinner, Kennedy read a telegram I gave him. "It's from my very generous Daddy. It says, 'Dear Son, I don't mind paying for your election, but I refuse to pay for a landslide.'" The laughs drowned out the problem and it never came up again. Kennedy laughed loudest when I said at one fund-raiser for him, "Why are you worried about winning? If you lose the U.S., you can always buy Europe."

If I did a joke in my column, "Strictly for Laughs," about JIMMY CARTER, the White House was ready to kill. All I said was, "Amy is taking skiing lessons because she wants to go downhill with her father." The next day I got a call from Washington, "Why are you picking on the President of the United States?"

I said on the air, "Carter says his anti-inflation program is working, the trouble is the people aren't." The next call from the White House said, "The President is distraught. What are you trying to prove?" I don't know why they got mad. All I said was, "I'm trying to prove that the President has a sense of humor like a social disease."

If you're going out for public office, you have to be able to take it as well as throw it, and nobody throws it better than RONALD REAGAN.

When I said, "Why do they say Reagan is too old to run for President just because his social security number is two?" R. R. called me personally. "Joey, this is Ron. What kind of crack is that about my age? I've got a funnier one. 'Why do they say I'm too old to be President just because my social security number is in Roman numerals?"

Reagan does it all with laughs. "The first time I ran for President I had to read for the part, but I'm going to run again now because I was always good at retakes—and better at sequels."

When JOHN ANDERSON said in one debate, "I'd rather be right than President," Reagan squelched, "Don't worry, you'll never be either."

When JIMMY CARTER said, "RONALD REAGAN is so far right he's on a bias," R. R. answered, "That's why Nancy likes to dance with me—I keep circling to the right."

When some people complained that Reagan was for the rich, he laughed back, "What's wrong with being rich? Listen, I've been rich and I've been poor and believe me, rich is better. Sure a lot of people got money to burn. Why not? It's cheaper than gas."

I told the President I had some great political jokes for him. He said, "I don't need them. I appointed plenty of my own."

At one dinner I announced, "I found a sure way for Reagan to stay in Washington. He lets it drop at a press conference that he plans to make more movies after he leaves the White House, whereupon the American people will immediately pass a constitutional amendment making him President for life."

Of course, the President had the last word. He said to me, "I don't know what I'd do without you, but I'm willing to try."

As Ronald Reagan says, "If we learn by our mistakes, we should have the best government on earth."

NELSON ROCKEFELLER had the greatest sense of humor of them all. He loved it when I picked on him. In fact, he insisted on it. He screamed the loudest when I said, "He's a self-made man. His father had billions but he treated Nelson like any normal kid. For Christmas he gave him a set of blocks—50th Street, 51st Street, 52nd Street. . . ."

At one big dinner at the Rainbow Room, Rockefeller asked me to be the toastmaster: "We will have the President, the Cardinal, a couple of dozen senators, Governor Reagan, Nixon, Agnew, and all the moneymen in town; it's got to be the dullest gathering of the year. So I want you to go to work on them. Roast them all, leave nobody out, and start with me."

Who am I to argue with the governor of my state? When Rockefeller introduced me, he said, "Okay, JOEY ADAMS, you're a comedian, tell us a joke." I said, "Okay, Nelson Rockefeller, you're a politician, tell us a lie." The governor laughed the loudest and we were off.

The first celebrity I introduced was TERENCE CARDINAL COOKE. "I better not make any jokes about his Eminence," I said. "The last time I did it, it snowed in my living room for three weeks."

I said to SPIRO AGNEW, "Your ability and sincerity have never been questioned, or even mentioned, come to think of it."

I introduced RICHARD NIXON as the greatest President: "That's not only my opinion, it's his, too. . . . Mr. Nixon is beginning to make noises like he'd like to run again. I suggest the border."

HENRY KISSINGER was next on my list: "Kissinger is a very religious man. He worships himself. . . . I hear he's changing his faith. He no longer believes he's God. . . . The only problem with Henry is, when you enter his office, you have to kiss his ring. I wouldn't mind, only he keeps it in his back pocket."

The laughs were coming fast and furious. "Now," I said, "the governor wants me to treat everybody equally. If I can pick on his Eminence, I can pick on anybody. After all, I have a right. I did a Catholic benefit last night. I know it was a Catholic benefit because I left my car in front of the hotel and they raffled it off."

"Now, let's take care of the Polish situation . . ." One man, in full dress, stood up in the center of the ballroom and shouted, "Before you go any further, Mr. Adams, I think you ought to know that *I am Polish.*" A hush came over the room. All the laughs were nothing now and the President, the governor, the entire audience sat there stunned. I said to the man, "I beg your pardon, what did you say?" He said again, but louder, "I want you to know that *I am Polish.*" I said, "That's okay. I'll speak slower." The audience screamed, the President banged the table, and Rockefeller threw his glass in the air. The crisis was over and a laugh was the cure again.

If you're going to run for office, I'm going to prepare you for everything but failure. A politician should keep his words soft, honeyed, and warm. He never knows when he might be called upon to eat them, so the funnier the better.

I learned that from my godfather, the late mayor of New York, FIORELLO LA GUARDIA. My "adopted father" turned chaos into harmony with one twist of humor. When one of his appointees stole some money, Fiorello went on the air and took full responsibility. "I very seldom make a mistake, but when I do it's a beaut." All was forgiven, even if the money wasn't returned.

La Guardia loved to laugh and he wanted everyone to do the same. During the newspaper strike in New York, the mayor went on the air to read the funnies to the kids. After he read DICK TRACY, he did his commercial: "And remember kids, dirty money never did anybody any good."

He didn't read the news, or the stock market report, or the weather. His one interest was to see that the kids, as well as the grownups, didn't lose the laughs.

There was a lot of talk when La Guardia married his secretary. It stopped when he grinned, "I lost a good secretary and gained a lousy cook."

A good laugh can get you out of any problem. When my good friend NELSON ROCKEFELLER was running for governor, his opponent was ARTHUR GOLDBERG. I thought it would be a good idea if Nelson went to the Borscht Belt with me, ate the cheese blintzes, danced with the Jewish ladies, and even stuffed himself with bagels, cream cheese, and lox.

He was a hit until the next day, when Arthur Goldberg called a press conference and said, "Rockefeller was compromising the Jews." It was a blow to my friend, who loved everyone. "What will I say?" he asked me. I said, "Let me answer when you hold the next press conference."

The first question was, "Did you hear Arthur Goldberg say you were compromising the Jews? Well?" Rocky said, "My pal Joey will answer that one." I said, "Goldberg is a nice Jewish man. My uncle Morris is also a nice Jewish man. My uncle shouldn't be governor and neither should Goldberg." The laughs drowned out his whole complaint.

I added, "Goldberg is the dullest speaker in the country. If he makes one more speech, Rockefeller will carry Canada."

LYNDON JOHNSON got his biggest laughs deprecating himself. He insisted that I give him a big intro so he could put himself down. I introduced him at Madison Square Garden one night as "the greatest President in the history of our country."

Johnson said, "My father would have loved that introduction, and my mother would have believed it. It's the greatest introduction I ever got. Except one time in Georgia, the governor was supposed to introduce me and he couldn't make it, so I introduced myself."

L.B.J. was another President who cloaked his political hide in a covering of wit. When Johnson decided against seeking a new term, thus becoming a hero overnight, he commented ruefully, "Sure, everybody loves his mother-in-law when she's leaving."

In his personal life, Johnson's humor expanded to accommodate his ego. One day he invited a group of pals to a barbecue on his ranch. Like all Texans, he was bragging: "I've got 3,000 head of cattle here." His neighbor interrupted. "Mr. President, I don't want to bring you down but every rancher in Texas has at least 3,000 head of cattle." And the President cracked, "In his refrigerator?"

L.B.J. had hundreds of phone numbers at the ready and he often dialed personally because he wanted fast answers.

Being preoccupied with lesser matters, such as the state of the Union, he wasn't clued into the fact that I had gotten into show business so I could sleep late.

"Mr. Adams, please," said President Johnson pleasantly when he called me one 11 A.M.

"He's asleep," answered my new Estonian housekeeper, whose first day on the job had come with instructions that I was not to be awakened before noon. Not by anybody. Not even by the President of the United States.

L.B.J. insisted. "This is the White House. It's important that I speak to Mr. Adams."

She answered: "Look, buster, I don't care what color is your house. I told you he's sleeping and I don't wake him for nobody. I wouldn't wake him for the President of the United States."

Johnson's voice rose. "This *is* the President." "So call back," she snapped and hung up.

Thirty minutes later I received the message that "Some president from a white house called." When I telephoned President Johnson, he uttered but one comment: "If there's ever a price on your head—take it!"

When I was a kid, I knew that all fairy tales began with the line, "Once upon a time." Now that I'm grown up, I know that all fairy tales begin with the line, "If I'm elected. . . ."

To be elected and live happily ever after today, the Good Fairy's tales had better be funny. Heavy-handed pols are learning that they need a good-humor man in the budget. It is for this reason that I have written this handbook of wit for politicians. Listen, if NIXON saved up jokes instead of tapes, he'd be a television star today.

They tell me now that Nixon was as sexy as KENNEDY. I just can't believe it. If Nixon had an affair in office, I misjudged him. I thought he was just doing it to the country.

Vice President GEORGE BUSH says, "The trouble with our foreign relations is that they're all broke."

There are thirty or forty basic political jokes, and all of them are running for President against REAGAN. There are so many Democratic candidates popping up, you'd think somebody fertilized the party. They're all calling for ammunition to laugh Reagan out of office. "In the latest poll, 50 percent of the American people don't want Reagan to run again. The other 50 percent want him to quit immediately." Reagan is always ready, at least his writers are always ready: "If the Democrats stop telling lies about us, then we'll stop telling the truth about them."

R. R. said, "I made so much money betting on the Democrats that I became a Republican."

The Democrats are loaded with ammunition too: "Reagan wants to run again, and he'll probably be elected. Sure, they always return to the scene of the crime."

Reagan always has the last laugh: "I haven't seen that much teamwork among the Democratic party in Washington since Congress voted itself a raise."

I supply the gags to all sides. May the one who gets the biggest laughs win: "REAGAN is so conservative he wants to change the Republican party symbol from an elephant to a dinosaur. He promises if he's reelected, he will legalize snuff."

I got Ronnie's answer: "If the Democrats get elected, it could be the dawn of a new error."

HENRY KISSINGER called Reagan a unique statesman. And everybody knows what a statesman is. That's a politician who never got caught.

Reagan said, "Henry reminds me of JOE NAMATH. Boy, can he throw it."

If you want to win by laughing them in or out of office, be my guest:

______ is a man who had greatness thrust upon him and ducked.

______ has done the work of two men—Laurel and Hardy.

______ has promised to help all the poor people. That's good, because if you vote for him, by next year we'll all be poor.

3
How to Take a Joke—No Matter Whose It Is

Laughter has eased the tensions of a troubled world ever since the days of the court jesters, through the ages of the wandering minstrels, the burlesque bananas, on through the sick comedians, and the roastmasters of today.

I'm going to give you the tools to sustain that laughter and show you how to use them for fun and profit. These notes do not distinguish between pro and amateur. When you are on your feet, *you* are the star, whether you're Bob Hope or the local bartender. It doesn't matter if the audience is twenty thousand at Madison Square Garden or two guys at a bar. You've got to live or die by yourself. But if you do it right, the laughter will sustain you, and I'm here to see that you do it right.

Mothers attempting to discover what makes an ordinary, happy, carefree boy become a comedian ask, "Where did he go wrong?" Is it the parents who have failed? How can they detect the early signs? If in infancy he grabs for the nurse instead of the rattle; if in kindergarten his favorite story is about the traveling salesman instead of Little Red Riding Hood; if in public school he's reading joke books instead of history books, they're in trouble.

Any comedian has a joke file where his brains should be. He's always at home when he's roasting somebody or getting roasted. The idea is to be able to take the gag and write it down to use on someone else.

You must always remember, there is no such thing as gentle humor. If you want to get laughs, you must be devastating, even if it's against yourself. A sense of humor is what makes you laugh at something that would make you mad if it happened to you.

That's the idea of this survival handbook for comics. When you throw the line, don't apologize, and when you're hit with the line, don't cry foul—laugh!

Taking Your Own Medicine

I always feel at home when I'm being roasted, and there's always some comic in residence at the Friars Club to make me feel at home: "I never miss your columns in the *Post*," BUDDY HACKETT said to me at a lunch. "I never see it so I never miss it."

MILTON BERLE welcomed me, "You're my favorite comedian, second only to Arafat." DON RICKLES was sweet: "Joey has always been a big help to people. So has Kaopectate."

SAMMY CAHN said, "You're okay in my book, but I only read dirty books." ALAN KING couldn't have been nicer. "JOEY ADAMS is a man who has no equals, only superiors."

SOUPY SALES sat down to be friendly: "I hear you're writing a new book called *The Joy of Cheap*. It's been so long since you paid for anything, you still don't know prices have gone up."

RED BUTTONS embraced me: "I hear your wife had a mirror installed over your bed because she likes to watch herself laugh." MICKEY ROONEY interrupted, "At least he gives his wife something to live for—a divorce."

Gee, it's really great to be at home at the Friars Club with friends.

ROBERT MERRILL stood up for me, "Don't pick on Joey Adams. He's been a member of the Friars since his demise some twelve years ago." JOHNNY CARSON said, "You're not yourself today, Joey, and I notice the improvement."

FRANK SINATRA was kind: "Joey is a good egg, and you know where eggs come from." MILTON BERLE noted, "In Joey's case, brain surgery would be a minor operation." BOB HOPE praised me: "Joey Adams is a legend in his own mind."

GEORGE BURNS passed without throwing one line. "Is George angry at me?" I asked HENNY YOUNGMAN. "Why?" he asked. "Well, he passed by without insulting me. Maybe he didn't see me?" Henny said, "He never *could* see you, but what the hell are you worrying about. *I* like you—I have no taste—but I like you."

When the comics get together and roast each other, it only means they love each other. We always roast the ones we love, and if you believe that, I have a condominium in El Salvador I'd love to unload on you.

Preparing for Battle

All these comics were ready with their rehearsed ad libs in case they ran into a target good for a laugh.

So, if you're going into battle, you've got to be prepared, and a good comic has to think funny twenty-four-hours a day. Who ever heard of a comedian who's only funny on Thursday?

A comic's job is the toughest. His option comes up after every joke, so he's got to be good each time out, and he's got to be prepared for any emergency. His brain becomes a computer with ready-to-use jokes for every occasion and every accident.

A plumber can't work without his tools. What is LIBERACE without his teeth, or LIZ TAYLOR without a husband? BOB HOPE is lost without his passport. And think of the case of DOLLY PARTON.

You sometimes hear a person say that he will speak "off the cuff," by which he means that his remarks will be impromptu. But the term "off the cuff" originally meant that the speaker had prepared himself, at least to some extent, by making notes on his shirt cuff, notes which he could easily read without seeming to.

I used to write my notes on my shirt cuff myself. However, I stopped when I heard my laundryman on the JOHNNY CARSON show one night doing my whole act. He was a big hit, too. No matter what your handicaps are as a speaker, they will be increased a hundredfold if you are not thoroughly prepared. If you are, many of your supposed handicaps will disappear. Don't rely on inspiration—ever. Be prepared, or prepare to run.

I once introduced BOB HOPE at a Boy Scout luncheon with a glowing eulogy that even he didn't believe. "After such an introduction," he said modestly, "I can hardly wait to hear what I have to say." But even the itinerant Hope wouldn't be so cockily confident if he weren't prepared for battle. All I'm trying to tell you is that you've got to do your homework if you want to pass the exam.

Ever since I started my column, "Strictly for Laughs," I have been receiving thousands of letters asking how to become a comedian. I talked to all my comic pals for the answers. MILTON BERLE says, "You take a mouthful of marbles and one by one you drop them. When you've lost all your marbles, you're a comedian."

JACKIE VERNON says: "A guy becomes a comedian like a girl becomes a prostitute. First he does it for fun, then for a few friends, and finally, he figures he might as well get paid for it."

I became a comedian when my father gave me a rocking chair. I loved that rocking chair. I used it day and night. One day it

broke, and when they discovered I was off my rocker,
was a comedian.

HENNY YOUNGMAN says, "If you want the real dope abou
comedy, come to the real dope."

HOPE says, "A comedian is a man who originates old jokes." BERLE says, "A comedian is a guy who knows a good gag when he steals one." And Berle is the hottest act in town. Every part is stolen.

I hope to show you in ten easy steps or twenty hard ones how to be the star of the dais, the roast, or the TV show. Or how to be the life of the party when you're asked to "say a few words."

1. Be funny. Leave the preaching to the rabbi, priest, or minister. Win your argument with a funny story instead of a sad one.
2. Be prepared. Don't be caught with your gags down and your mouth open without anything to say.
3. Use the joke or the gag that fits and fits you.
4. Practice. Every day. On the butcher, the baker, or the candlestick maker's wife.
5. Personalize your stories. Name the characters and the place.
6. Be brief. The mind cannot accept what the seat cannot endure.
7. Laugh at yourself. Use yourself or your family as the butt.
8. Use the gag file to find the subject or the jokes you want and then apply it to your target.
9. Switch the gag if necessary to give it a custom fit.
10. Memorize the "savers"; they may save you from sure death.

Savers

No comedian, public speaker, or master of ceremonies should be without "savers." They are the gags that save your life when you're dying, and although every gag can't always be a scream, the saver can turn it into a winner.

I know you're not going to believe it, but even I have laid a bomb with a joke here and there in my long career in show business. When things are going a little rough for me—which is very rare, it says here—my saver usually is, "Are you sure Bob Hope started this way?"

Some comics have built their act on savers: "I started at the bottom, and after this show I'll stay there!"

"Is this an audience or a jury?"

"My mother said I would come out on top. She's right—I'm getting bald!"

"Before I came out here I was a comer. Now I'm a goner."

Is it a particularly quiet audience, especially after your best gag? "What time do you want to be called in the morning?"

Are you really in trouble?: "I don't have to do this for a living. I could always starve!"

Savers can change disaster into victory. When a joke goes wrong: "We will now pause for thirty seconds of silence for that joke that just died."

If two jokes die in a row: "I bet when I came out you thought I was going to be lousy."

After the third bomb: "Just give me a ten yard head start."

I saved my own life after five minutes of silence (and I was using my best gags). "This could be worse," I said. "I could be here in person."

HENNY YOUNGMAN defuses his bombs with, "I want to thank you for coming to my funeral."

MILTON BERLE: "Ever get the feeling you're in the wrong business?"

BOB HOPE: "Please come back to see me again, but not as a group."

My favorite saver, the one that never fails, is the sympathy line. "I have a little boy at home who is all alone. I'm the only one he has in the whole world. And when I come home at night, he rushes up to me and says, 'Daddy, were you a big hit tonight? Did they laugh, daddy? Did they, huh?' And if I have to tell him I was a flop, it would break his heart. So your laughs and your applause and maybe a standing ovation are not for me, really, they're for that poor little kid who is sitting at home alone, just waiting to hear how I did tonight."

Laugh Lines

If you listen to me, I can make you the talker of the town. You know BERLE? Big star? He listened to me. GEORGE BURNS. Great monologist? He listened to me. BOB HOPE listened to me. HENNY YOUNGMAN? He didn't listen.

Now you need the jokes. Let's steal, I mean borrow—that is, sample—the jokes of the masters. Just take the ones that fit you or fit the occasion. Come to think of it, you might as well take them all. You never know when you'll need them.

Do you need age jokes? GEORGE BURNS is the master. He claims to be an expert on diet, exercise, and sex. "Well, two out of three ain't bad." Says George, "I am just as good now with girls as I ever was—and I was very bad then."

George preaches: "Sex can be fun after eighty, after ninety, and after lunch." George describes: "Old age is when it takes you all night to do what you used to do all night."

"You're eighty-seven, I said to George. "How do you do it, I mean sexwise?" He said, "I don't want to leave you with the impression that I'm always out with young girls. That's not true. Sometimes I stay home with them."

PHYLLIS DILLER admits she has a tremendous sex drive: "My boyfriend lives forty miles away." Phyllis gets her biggest laughs by putting herself down: "They caught a peeping Tom outside my bedroom window—sleeping."

Phyllis told me, "I was going with a very handsome, rich, sexy guy. He ran away with another woman, so I left him."

RODNEY DANGERFIELD gets no respect. "The superintendent in my building tells me to wipe my feet in my apartment before I go out in the hall." Rodney cries, "Even as a kid I got no respect. I was kidnapped when I was a kid. The ransom note said, 'Pay us five thousand or you'll see your kid again!'"

LOU JACOBI gives advice to his listeners: "To get along in today's economy a man should have something working for him, like a wife."

A MYRON COHEN classic: Two retired traveling salesmen are discussing the old days on the road. "Do you think there's as much sex going on now as there used to be?" asks one. "Sure," says the other, "but there's a new crowd doing it."

MORTY GUNTY says he worked in a show with a belly dancer who got herself tattooed because her boyfriend said he liked moving pictures.

RED SKELTON asked the Scotsman, "Hey Jack, is anything worn under the kilt?" He answered, "Certainly not. Everything is in perfect working order."

JOAN RIVERS' favorite target is ELIZABETH TAYLOR: "Did you hear? Her thighs are going condo!"

Don't try to stop MILTON BERLE. Just memorize. I go back a long way with Milton, and his jokes go back even further: Do you know what it means to come home to a woman who'll give you a little love, a little affection, a little tenderness? It means you're in the wrong house. It takes my wife forty minutes to get her lipstick on. You know why? Because she's got a big mouth, that's why."

Milton is proud to say, "I saved a girl from being attacked last night. I controlled myself."

NORM CROSBY is an authority on marriage: "I'm not illiterate. My parents were married, and *I* married kind of late in life. That's because when I was younger I couldn't find a girl who liked to do the same things I liked to do. I liked to hang around the pool room, drink beer, and chase girls. I couldn't find a girl who would do all those things with me."

Sex is a big topic for the comics—especially the ladies. Gone are the days when the little woman was seen and not heard. Today, she's obscene and heard pretty good. Take mighty mouth JOAN RIVERS: "Sex with love is about the most beautiful thing there is; but sex without love isn't so bad either."

PHYLLIS DILLER says, "What sex life? I went to the Virgin Islands and they gave me a hero's welcome!"

MARILYN SOKOL confides, "Men are after one thing, and one thing only, and for that I say, *Hallelujah!*"

ARLENE DAHL: "The reason I don't make movies today is that in the old days actresses used to *play* parts. Now they reveal them."

HELEN GURLEY BROWN: "My husband's every waking thought is

of sex. Unfortunately, as soon as he is through thinking about it, he goes to sleep."

MARILYN MICHAELS: "Never make love to a man when you have something better to do. But what's better?"

Sex therapists are all over the air, giving advice on how to do it. My friends aren't interested in *how to*—they want to know *who with*? One caller asked DR. ELLEN SIROKA on NBC, "Who says hookers have it easy? How would you like to get dressed all the time just to go on a coffee break?"

An hysterical girl called DR. RUTH WESTHEIMER: "You've got to help me. I love him. He loves me. We like the same things. When we're apart we're miserable. I don't know what to do." The doctor said, "I don't get it. You sound like you're completely compatible and in love. What's the problem?" The girl said, "What's the problem? The problem is what shall I tell my husband?"

This guy called the sexologist and cried, "My timing is terrible. Now that the sexual revolution has arrived, I seem to have run out of ammunition." She explained, "Sex is good for everything. Doctors now say that sex is even good for relieving arthritis symptoms." He said, "But I don't have arthritis." She said, "Haven't you heard of preventive medicine?"

A girl called the sex therapist and said, "Remember when you told me the way to a man's heart was through his stomach?" The therapist said, "Yes, I remember." The girl went on, "Well, last night I found a new route. Now I need some birth control pills." The doc asked, "What's his occupation?" She said, "Army." The doc asked, "Active or retired?" She said, "If he wasn't active I wouldn't need these bloody pills, would I?"

This girl called the station and asked for the sex expert and explained, "My sex life has improved immeasurably since my husband and I got twin beds." The sexologist asked, "How could that be?" She said, "Well, his is in Connecticut and mine is in Manhattan."

A girl said, "This bum took me to a movie, then to a nice restaurant, then to his apartment for a few drinks. Did I do wrong?" The doc asked, "Don't you remember?" She explained, "Well, he made love to me against my will." The therapist asked, "Didn't you respond or embrace him also?" She replied, "Yes, I did it only in self-defense!"

Marriage is a great subject for the comics. WOODY ALLEN says: "I tended to place my wife under a pedestal. After ten years I finally got something to quiet my nerves—a divorce."

RIP TAYLOR: "Our marriage is at an awkward stage. She wants to see a marriage counselor, and I want to see a hit man."

BURT REYNOLDS: "Marriage is about the most expensive way for the average man to get his laundry done."

MILTON BERLE: "My wife practices the rhythm method. That means she won't make love unless there's a drummer in the room."

BILL COSBY: "In Iran, kissing for pleasure is now called a crime. In America, kissing without pleasure is called marriage."

SOUPY SALES: The matchmaker in Israel said to the young man, "I have a girl for you with $20,000." The chap said, "Can I see her picture?" The matchmaker replied, "With $20,000 we don't show pictures."

PHYLLIS DILLER: "My husband took me to a wife-swapping party, and he had to throw in some cash."

DOLLY PARTON: "The night of our honeymoon my husband took one look and said, 'Is that all for me?'"

RONALD REAGAN: "Everybody is always asking me for advice on married life. Maybe because I'm the boss in my family. Whatever I say goes. The only trouble is, when I raise my hand, my wife never calls on me."

WARREN BEATTY: "I think arguments are healthy between men and women. If you use them right they help prevent marriage.... My biggest criticism of my friend Frank is that he doesn't plan and think ahead. He's getting married next month and he hasn't tried to find a job for his wife."

Some people have all the luck when it comes to successful marriages. MICKEY ROONEY has had eight of them, ZSA ZSA and LIZ TAYLOR seven each. My neighbor asks, "If we got married for better or for worse, when does the better come?" JOAN RIVERS says, "The only happy couple I know is DOLLY PARTON."

You know the honeymoon is over when your wife says she's going to slip into something more comfortable, and it turns out to be a twin bed. She said, "I can no longer trust my husband, he is so deceitful. He pretends to believe me when he knows I'm lying to him."

A successful man is one who earns more than his wife can spend; a successful woman is one who finds such a man. "Of course my wife and I are compatible," a man told his analyst. "In fact, we both like the same thing. It's just that I like to save it and she likes to spend it." Another man says, "I told my wife, 'This town ain't big enough for both your credit cards.'"

Marriage is often like a boxing card. The preliminaries are usually better than the main event. She was nagging him as usual. "This is the last straw," she threatened, "I'm going to divorce you." Her long-suffering mate smiled weakly, "Now, dear," he murmured, "I know you don't mean it. You're just saying it to make me feel good."

"I can't stand him for another minute," she screamed. "He gets drunk, spends all our money on gambling and other women, and if he comes home at all, it's just to change clothes." The lawyer said, "It certainly looks like you have grounds for divorce." She hollered, "Divorce? I should say not! I've lived with that bum for fifty years. *Now* I should make him happy?"

Two secretaries were discussing the attributes of their ideal husbands. The first one insisted that her ideal mate be musically inclined, sing, dance, tell jokes, and, above all, stay home with her every night. Her friend said, "Are you sure you want to get married? You're better off with a TV set."

The All-Occasion Antidote

My prescription for laughter is to supply you with jokes, gags, and stories for any and all occasions:

Are you facing a room full of doctors? "It's true a doctor will always take care of poor people, even if it means making you one.... I was a little upset when my doctor charged me $500 and told me I'm going to have to live with it. That's like a hooker telling you to take a cold shower."

Is the dentist your guest of honor? "The modern dentist lives up to his claim: It won't hurt a bit—until the bill comes." I said to my dentist, "You may be a painless dentist, but this is going to hurt a little. I don't have the money." DOCTOR CUOZZO told me he was so embarrassed: "DOLLY PARTON came in and asked me to examine her teeth." Naturally, I asked what happened. He said, "Nothing. I couldn't reach them."

Is dieting your subject for today? Medical scientists say sex burns up 100 calories. To lose 10 pounds a week, do you know what that means? "I'm a little wary of those dieting supplements that are supposed to increase your sex drive. I know a guy who took Vitamin E and his wife took iron pills. Now when he's ready, she's rusty."

Then there's the Methuselah diet:

> Methusaleh ate what was on his plate,
> Not as people do now.
> He never took a calorie count,
> He ate it because it was chow.
> He cheerfully chewed his food
> Unmindful of troubles or fears
> Lest his health might be hurt
> By some fancy dessert
> And he lived over nine hundred years.

Laugh and the world laughs with you—but only if the jokes are good:

Government

With the state of the world today, the only one who's in good shape is BO DEREK. Everybody knows what our world leaders say, so why repeat it? I bring you the news that you don't read about: Did you know the White House plans to take action against Japan's car exports? It will close all karate schools in the United States. REAGAN told a labor meeting he's pro unions. He's pro unions like Nancy is pro Woolworths.

Special news bulletin: The NIXON library finally found a home in San Clemente. They won't charge any admission—you have to break in. The Secretary of Defense doesn't want REAGAN to cut the budget because "We'll need all the guns and tanks we can get to stop the senior citizens when they march on Washington." The Democrats are also bothered by inflation. Instead of three top candidates for the Presidency, they now have nine.

If we learn by our mistakes, we should have the best government on Earth. Congress voted itself a raise. They had to because since ABSCAM, the FBI cut out giving bribes. It's not nice to call people liars—that's why we call them congressmen. The Congress says it wants to raise our hopes for a better life. For a better life I don't need my hopes raised. I need my taxes lowered.

A lot of women's groups have asked NANCY REAGAN to influence her husband's ideas on the nuclear arms build-up. And she has. We first knew about it when President Reagan stunned a press conference the other day by announcing his support for a new line of designer missiles. Listen, the Reagans paid $292,616 in taxes this year and Nancy is upset. She could have used that money for a new dress.

More and more congressmen now stay in Washington all year round because they can't live at home under the laws they've passed. There's still a double standard. The place where a woman sells herself is called a house of ill repute. The place where a man sells himself is called the House of Representatives.

REAGAN explains his policy: "Charity begins at home, but why does it have to wind up in every foreign country?"

GEORGE BUSH says, "The trouble with foreign aid is, it allows too many nations to live beyond our means."

I got the jokes and the gags to get them all in and out of trouble and in and out of office—which is the same thing. I'm not taking sides. All I can say is, may the best man win. The trouble is, he's not running this year.

4

The Roast of the Town—Laugh Prescriptives

In this era of masochistic comedy, our most famous personalities have accepted testimonials in their honor, just to be carved to pieces by their murderous confreres.

The idea of these roasts is, if you can't say anything nice about the guy, let's hear it.

These murderers don't get the chair unless it's the center one on some dais to trigger the slaughter of a poor suspecting guest. The honored one is sworn to take it. The question is, can you give it? That's what I'm here for—to arm you with the appropriate ammunition.

BOB HOPE said about DEAN MARTIN, "Dean is the most relaxed performer on TV. He never spills a word." JOHNNY CARSON said about DON RICKLES, "What can you say about Don that hasn't been said about warts?" Rickles about Carson: "Johnny has become a household word. Garbage is also a household word."

You see what I mean? At these dinners, we are the original believers in equal opportunity. We cut up everybody equally. I said to RICKLES, "There's only one thing that keeps me from breaking you in half. I don't want two of you." Don belted me, "JOEY ADAMS is the kind of guy I'd like to have over when I have the measles."

These dais assassins spare nobody. At the roast for eighty-seven-year-old GEORGE BURNS, FRANK SINATRA took the first shot: "George's love life is a little strange these days. I've heard of guys taking a nap *before* sex. Some take a nap *after* sex. But George, during it?"

SAMMY DAVIS, JR., kissed George. "George is at the age now where his back goes out more then he does." BOB HOPE said, "JOHN PHILLIP SOUSA played at his senior prom."

ALAN KING said, "Would you believe he's still chasing girls—if it's down hill. At his age he can't take 'yes' for an answer."

HOWARD COSELL: "GEORGE BURNS is trying to prove that his sex life is just as good as it never was."

FRANK SINATRA, the Abbot of the Friars, sat on the firing line at one big dinner. MILTON BERLE fired first. "Frankie boy, if only your zipper could talk."

LUCILLE BALL said, "Sinatra leads a full life. Never a dull moment. Even when he went to church, four or five priests would crowd into the confessional booth. It isn't often that a confession gets applause."

RED BUTTONS: "FRANK SINATRA is an antique relic of yesteryear. He is the PAUL ANKA of the menopause set."

CARY GRANT was honest. "On my feet I cease to function. To tell the truth, I can't function when I'm lying down either. That's why I love your style, Frank."

BERLE hollered, "I'll tell you one thing about Sinatra. No one has ever been turned away from his door—*if* you're over twenty-one and have big knockers."

DON RICKLES: "Everything Sinatra touches turns to gold. I'm afraid to go to the toilet with him. . . . I'll tell you how big Frank is," Don said. "He wears a cross in nobody's honor. . . . Frank has never let anything put him down. Once he went to visit a little old man in a hospital in Hoboken, and he sang to the poor soul for an hour. When he finished, he said to him, 'I hope you get better,' and the little old man said, 'you too!'"

I said, "Frank, when it was announced that this was a dinner in your honor, everybody fought to be on the dais. Those who won aren't here."

BOB HOPE said, "GEORGE BURNS wanted to be here tonight but something came up—and he was very proud." Bob said, "When Sinatra plays Vegas, all the beautiful women in the audience throw their hotel keys on the stage. When I play there they throw their room keys at me, too, but after they check out."

DON RICKLES explains, "We play it strictly for laughs. We don't want to leave any scars." Don claims only one person ever objected to his needling. "I made fun of a ringsider's beard and almost got belted. That broad had no sense of humor."

Don said to HENNY YOUNGMAN, "I think the world of you—and you know what I think of the world."

Rickles has his own version of the WILL ROGERS line: "I never met a man I couldn't dislike. . . . LIBERACE came to California for arthritis thirty years ago—and he's finally got it."

"ED MCMAHON is a lot of fun, if you like to yawn."

To ERNEST BORGNINE, "Look at your face! Was anyone else hurt in the accident?"

To ORSON WELLES, "Who makes those tents you wear?"

"DEAN MARTIN has finally solved his drinking problem. He wears an old suit in case he falls down."

To PAT BOONE, "I bet you think your pimples come from eating too many Hersheys."

To WAYNE NEWTON, "Wayne, I've seen you in nightclubs, I've watched you in movies, I've listened to your records, and I say this from my heart. *You're dull.*"

To BURT REYNOLDS, "Burt, in my book you have the sexual attractiveness of a dentist's drill."

On stage Don is the merchant of venom, the master maligner. Actually, he is a very gentle man until he faces an audience, and then he makes ARAFAT sound like a Boy Scout. But as soon as the battle is over, he takes them home for chicken soup to help them get well.

Recently, Don's victims turned the tide of battle and ran a dinner in his dishonor, where the boys exploded their biggest bombs. Naturally, being his pest friend, I started it. "Don married a good girl, a sentimental girl. She saw a sign 'help the handicapped' so she married him."

RED BUTTONS: "I understand Rickles went to Lebanon recently and sold the Arabs the rights to the perfect bomb—his TV show."

JACK CARTER: "Don's the kind of guy that would buy his mother a swimming pool in Florida—and put sharks in it."

SINATRA was loving: "Don was so ugly when he was born, the doctor slapped his mother."

BOB HOPE: "There's one thing that can be said about Don Rickles—but I don't use that kind of language."

JOHNNY CARSON:"Rickles will always work—if there's no one around with talent."

ORSON WELLES: "Underneath Rickles' rough exterior there really is a rabid shark."

DEAN MARTIN: "Don Rickles is the greatest comic in the world. He is the funniest and the nicest man I know. But you know, I'm drunk, and when I'm drunk I'm the biggest liar in the world."

JACKIE GLEASON: "Don has all the charm of an earthquake. Every night he puts out the cat—with ether."

Now, take HENNY YOUNGMAN—*please.* If it weren't for pick-pockets he wouldn't have any sex life at all. MILTON BERLE said, "Henny, as a young man, came from a poor but stupid family."

SHECKY GREEN introduced JERRY LEWIS as "the only man I know who ever had a paternity suit filed against him by his own children."

"MICKEY ROONEY had an unhappy childhood. When he was five he ran away from home. The police came and his parents couldn't describe him."

BOB HOPE said, "PHYLLIS DILLER is a ten—nine in the rear and one in the chest."

JOAN RIVERS: "LIZ TAYLOR has been married so many times she has rice marks on her face."

JACK CARTER to MOREY AMSTERDAM: "I was going to bring you a present—but what do you give a man who has nothing?"

I introduced SPIRO AGNEW as a very humble man—"and he's got a lot to be humble about."

I introduced JOHNNY CARSON: "Success hasn't changed him. He's still the same arrogant bastard he always was."

Now it was time to pin the tail on me. The roast is the highest tribute you can give a guest of honor these days. It's not necessary to give him a hand. A finger will do.

In fact, I preferred it, when the boys got together recently, to squeeze a grapefruit and me. I laughed the loudest when BOB HOPE said, "Joey is a goodwill ambassador for the President in Asia. I saw him recently in Vietnam. He's so popular there, they were shooting at him from both sides."

If you were to take a bunch of comedians of different sizes, styles, and shapes and shove them into a room, you'd probably go nuts—which is what happened when the boys gave me a dinner to dishonor me as America's goodwill ambassador.

HENNY YOUNGMAN: "Joey would be more popular if he were as well known as his jokes."

MILTON BERLE: "Joey claims he's a self-made man. Next time I hope he calls in somebody else."

MYRON COHEN: "Joey is one of the most sought-after men in the country—for income tax evasion."

STEVE ALLEN: "This boy has a lot of talent—but it's in his wife's name."

DON RICKLES: "Joey lights up a room—by leaving it."

JAN MURRAY swept onstage furious. "I don't understand this whole bit," he fumed. "Who the hell elected him Man of the Year? Who voted? We started out together. I'm better looking than he. I have a daily TV show. He's made Man of the Year and I can't even get chosen Jew of the block. Don't you think it's a little incongruous?" By now he's screaming. "They gave this little jerk a big dinner at the Waldorf and BERNARD BARUCH sat on a park bench by himself. Don't you think it's blasphemous, when Joey gets a plaque and ALBERT SCHWEITZER's trophy room is empty?" He steamed off yelling: "I'd like to say something nice about my friend JOEY ADAMS—but I just can't think of it."

I knew my dear wife, CINDY, would save me. And she did—for the knockout: "We've been wed a long time," she said, "and I think married life is wonderful. It's just Joey I can't stand. Of course, many people thought our marriage wouldn't last because my husband is so much older than I. I don't think he's so old at all, although recently he did receive a brochure from an old age home and it was marked 'urgent.' I find it hard to forget Joey is the world's foremost authority on humor today. So would you if you had to write it on the blackboard five hundred times before you got your first mink coat."

I asked DON RICKLES, after all the insults and the putdowns, if there was anybody he really hates. He said, "No, I wouldn't say it if there was. My style is to rib people I *like*. If there's anger in it, it isn't funny. But you must remember, it must be funny. Good taste and humor are a contradiction in terms—like a chaste whore!"

The big consolation the target has is that they never give you a dinner until you can afford to buy your own. Notice, please, that the killers only pick on the giants who are trained to take it and who are big enough to defend themselves.

I hope you also noticed that they never pick on anybody's physical handicaps, like his glasses or his bald head or the size of his nose or his body—unless it is for good instead of evil. For instance, if you want to win a bald man's heart: "God made a lot of heads, and those he was ashamed of he put a lot of hair on." If he's a little guy: "He saves a lot of money. He walks under the turnstiles." Or "He's so cute. He sits down and stands up, he's the same size."

The important thing to remember is that the roast must fit the roastee. You can't do drunk jokes about the Cardinal, no matter how good the gag is. And you can't do religious lines about DEAN MARTIN, no matter how sacred.

If you say, "Dean Martin is not relaxed, he's just limp from being boozed up—you could build a skating rink with the ice cubes he uses in his drink," sure it's funny. But not if you apply it to the Cardinal.

However, if you say, "His Eminence is so religious, Dean shook hands with him and his entire right side sobered up," it's on target.

I said about NELSON ROCKEFELLER, "This man is so rich he has a solid gold bathtub. When he leaves the bath, he leaves 14-carat rings."

Obviously, this wouldn't fit the taxicab driver or your maid, but you can switch it to the president of your bank, the head of the studio, or your favorite Gabor.

If you are talking about SOPHIA LOREN and you say, "She is so sexy that the birds and the bees study *her*," you know you are on the ball. But you know you can't do this same line with PHYLLIS DILLER or DON RICKLES.

Do you know what TWIGGY has printed on her chest? "In case of attack: this side up." Of course, you can't use this one on DOLLY PARTON. However, how's this for Dolly: "I bumped into her the other day—she was across the street at the time. . . . It must be terrible having to wear a bra with heavy-duty shocks. . . . Dolly says you miss a lot by being built that way. On stage you can't see what's going on in the first three rows." You can switch to LONI ANDERSON, or RACQUEL WELCH, or BO DEREK, or SOPHIA LOREN.

JACKIE ONASSIS is having a terrible operation. They're going to remove her navel. She's putting in a wall safe.

ZSA ZSA says she only marries for love—and she'll keep getting married till she finds it. This is a good line for ELIZABETH TAYLOR or MICKEY ROONEY as well. Baseball is our national pastime. Now go convince Zsa Zsa or Liz or Mickey.

Are you attacking a newspaperman? "He once drove a cab. He must have—he's a hack writer."

Are you giving it to a doctor? "Doctor Schwartz just told me he's divorcing his wife. Every time he got in bed, she handed him an apple."

Is a lawyer your target? "He's a great attorney. He's willing to spend your last cent to prove he's right."

Are you ready to take on the sports celebrities? Here are some Rickles razzberries.

To HOWARD COSELL: "Next time you buy a toupee, get one with brains in it."

To MUHAMMAD ALI: "He was born at home, but when his mother saw him she went to the hospital."

"KAREEM ABDUL JABBAR, the Los Angeles basketball star, is a great friend to have if you happen to live on the second floor and lose your keys."

To GEORGE STEINBRENNER: "Make yourself at home. Hit somebody, or fire somebody."

"NOLAN RYAN takes those walks around the mound so he can have time to figure out if Houston doesn't win the pennant what kind of work he'll be out of."

"TOMMY LASORDA, the manager of the Los Angeles Dodgers, hangs out with FRANK SINATRA because Tommy has an uncle who's being held hostage in Italy. . . . The reason Tommy's belly is so big is so if the Dodgers blow the pennant he can tie a cord around his neck and work as a balloon."

"JOE NAMATH's a great guy to invite to a party. Sits in a corner and pumps up footballs. . . . Joe wore white shoes during his playing days because right after the game he'd hop a plane to Miami to dance with old broads in rest homes."

"LEE TRAVINO is a great golfer, except during the lettuce festival. Then he falls apart."

"JACK NICKLAUS's idea of an exciting night is to hang around a ball wash."

"People make jokes about the fact that CARL YASTRZEMSKI is Polish. I see no humor in that, especially when Yaz crashes into the fence at Fenway Park on days when there's no game going on."

"JOE MORGAN doesn't really twitch when he's in the batter's box. He's just trying out his sense of rhythm in case he decides to become a tap dancer."

I'll give you the putdowns. Stick any one of them in anybody. Just make sure it belongs or that it can do harm; that is, put it where it'll get the biggest laugh.

His show is closing this week. The reviews were good, but the word-of-mouth killed it.

I hope you jump on a bicycle and discover it has no seat.

I came here tonight to pay tribute to a great human being. And after I pay tribute, I'll say a few words about our guest of honor.

Are you roasting the head of a union? "Harold is a great labor leader—he's put more girls in labor than any man in the movement."

The thing to remember is that a roast that is rare or medium rare is not as effective as one that is well done. But, keep moving when you throw them—unless you enjoy being a target.

Here are some devastating lines. Apply where necessary:

Talk about trouble? He walks in his sleep and he sleeps in the nude.

Fat? He qualifies for group insurance.

His parents didn't like him. His bath toys were a radio and a toaster.

Some surgeon. He moonlights as a chef in a Japanese restaurant. When he got married, nobody would give the bride away—they finally held an auction.

When he was in school he received a letter in football. It said, "Return your equipment."

He's a graduate of Harvard—where he crammed four years into seven.

He hasn't an enemy in the world—he's outlived them all.

To most girls he's a father figure. They keep asking him for money.

He comes from a town so small, the local hooker was the community chest.

He's a little shook up. His wife told him she wants to have sex in the back seat of the car, and she wants *him* to drive.

He's a great lover. The other night he was making love to his wife, and she lost the place in her book twice.

I wouldn't give away his age but his New York City birth certificate is written in Dutch.

He always had a great way with the ladies. It's expensive—but it's a way.

He can remember the night he lost his innocence in the back seat of the family car. It would have been even more memorable if he hadn't been alone.

Our guest of honor drastically cut down his cigarette consumption. He only smokes after sex.

He's a comedy writer for ARAFAT and the AYATOLLAH KHOMEINI.

POLLUTION: Remember when the air was clean and sex was dirty? My apartment has lots of windows—so I get cross pollution. . . . Despite the pollution, New York gets in your blood—and in your hair and on your clothes.

PROSTITUTION: Why is everybody knocking the Broadway prostitutes? That's the only industry that isn't leaving New York.

TAXES: The government must really need money. I heard the IRS is now selling gift certificates. . . . I'm putting all my money in taxes. It's the only thing sure to go up.

WOMEN'S LIB: I'm glad my wife joined women's lib. Now she complains about *all* men—not just me. . . . My secretary just joined women's lib to find her real identity, which is ridiculous. She wears a wig, false eyelashes, and a padded bra.

INDIANS: Do you realize the Indians are the only ones ever to be conquered by the United States and not come out ahead?

FASHION: Women will be wearing the same thing in brassieres this year. . . . If women dressed to please their husbands, they'd wear last year's clothes. . . . Overheard in local boutique: "But, Madam, looking ridiculous is the fashion this year."

Lawyers

Lawyers can now advertise—like the butcher, the baker, and the plumber who overcharges.

The man who said "talk is cheap" never hired a lawyer.

The Attorney General has determined that your lawyer may be hazardous to your wealth.

The defendant said, "I don't need a lawyer. I intend to tell the truth."

Love will always find a way—but if it doesn't, her attorney will.

You can't live without lawyers, and you sure can't die without them.

I've known lawyers who sometimes tell the truth. They'll do anything to win a case.

For Doctors Only

The credo of the men of medicine: Always write your prescriptions illegibly and your bill plainly.

House calls are now made only by burglars.

Most doctors are fair. They don't operate unless they need the money.

A doctor will never violate his oath—the oath he took to become a millionaire.

There's an advantage in being poor. A doctor will cure you faster.

A doctor will tell you that if you give up drinking, smoking, desserts, and chasing women, you can look forward to a long, boring life.

You're just what the doctor ordered—a patient with a good credit rating.

With the price of apples today, you're better off with a doctor.

I'm worried about going to see a doctor when I realize doctors are usually described as practicing.

Sign in doctor's office: The doctor is very busy. Have your symptoms ready.

An apple a day keeps the doctor away. So does not paying your bill.

Americans spent $25 billion on medicine last year—which proves that a lot of doctors are feeling no pain.

I went to see my doctor about my loss of memory. He made me pay in advance.

We have a family physician—he treats mine and I support his.

Politicians

The politician is the easiest target. He approaches every subject with an open mouth. Every politician says he talks straight from the shoulder—too bad his words don't start from higher up. . . . Listen, if half the statements of opposing politicians are true, none of these guys are fit to hold public office.

Now that RONALD REAGAN is assured the nomination for a second term, you can bet that Congress will pass a law that everyone has to be home by 11 P.M. so they can watch his old movies on television. . . . Reagan says, although he does not support the ERA, he believes in equal rights for women. That's like being against sex, but *for* motherhood.

I think MONDALE is the man to get this country moving again. I know if he came into *my* neighborhood, *I'd* move.

Some people think our Presidents should be limited to a single six-year term. Personally, I think all politicians should be given six-year terms—with possible time off for good behavior.

Advice to congressmen: Never take a bribe from an Arab who has blue eyes and a crew cut. . . . And if you think what those congressmen did was a crime—how about the raise they voted for themselves?

GEORGE BUSH's big issue is inflation: "The interest rates are so high that if JOHN DILLINGER were alive today, he wouldn't rob a bank—he'd open one."

Are you interested in dissecting the UN? "The UN says it keeps the peace. I guess so. In twenty-five years there has never been a war in that building. . . . The idea of the UN was to make all nations act like friends. So far they're all acting like relatives. . . . Members of the UN will not tolerate injustice and oppression—except at home."

Whether you're a politician, a comic, a businessman, or an actor, you've got to laugh at it—no matter how sick the joke is—and you'll laugh yourself well.

The Cure for Hecklers

The show business fraternity has left longer lasting scars on hecklers than Zorro. Every circle has a square who is "funnier than the guy on stage" until "the guy on stage" puts him back in the woodwork where he belongs. So, if you're heckled on stage or at a party or at work, don't get angry—get funny. Don't get ulcers—get laughs. Just don't fool around with the pros. This is their business and they are prepared to give it to you any time you ask for it.

Play your own version of Pin the Tail on the Donkey. Face the jackass and pin the joke on him: "You have a nice personality, but not for a human being."

MILTON BERLE was challenged by a small-timer at the Carnegie Delicatessen. "You want to have a battle of wits?" Miltie asked. "I'll check my brains and we'll start even."

"Ya bum," one heckler screamed at DON RICKLES, "I'll put you in my back pocket." Don said, "Then you'll have more brains in your pocket than you have in your head."

You don't have to be a pro to handle the heckler when you're on stage or on a dais or with the party pest. Here are some of my favorite answers, with muscles guaranteed to flatten the toughest opponent and get the biggest laughs. Don't get upset if they walk out on you. It's when they walk toward you that you have to worry:

- In your case brain surgery would be a minor operation.
- One good way to save face is to keep the lower half shut.

- I don't know what I'd do without you, but I'm willing to tı
- There's a bus leaving in ten minutes—get under it.
- Find yourself a home in a wastebasket.
- If you had your life to live over again, don't do it.
- Do you have a chip on your shoulder—or is that your head?
- I hear they just redecorated your home—put new padding on the walls.
- Say, you're a regular C.P.A.—a constant pain in the ass.
- Some day you'll go too far and I hope you stay there.
- I won't ask you to act like a human being. I know you couldn't do imitations.
- Why don't you phone me sometime so I can hang up on you.

SAMMY DAVIS, JR., said to a pest, "If you're ever in California, sir, I do hope you'll come to my house and use my pool. I'd like to give you some drowning lessons."

The noisy diner was banging on the table. "The service here is lousy," he yelled. "Look at my glass. It's empty. What does a guy have to do to get some water around here?" The waiter answered, "Why don't you set fire to yourself?"

Use these heckle lines with confidence, but wait till you get it; then the audience or party or table is with you.

- If you have something to say—shut up.
- Sir, you are annoying the man I love.
- Sir, some day you'll find yourself—and will you be disappointed.

The art of insult has replaced the art of self-defense. Only make sure you're a David when you sling mud at a Goliath. Keep moving—don't be a target.

The pros are always ready. You can be, too, if you memorize

some of these lines—but only use them if they fit and if the insult to you was strong enough to make their use warranted.

The bar was unusually noisy one evening when JOE E. LEWIS was doing his show at the Copa. Joe drawled, "They redecorated the bar. They put new drunks around it."

SONNY KING was interrupted all through his favorite ballad by a coughing and sneezing drunk. "No wonder this guy has a cold," he sneered. "He's got a hole in his head."

JOEY BISHOP, to a celebrity heckler: "Do you mind if I have you X-rayed? I want to see what they see in you."

Taking care of female hecklers is a little more delicate but not less devastating:

- She's the kind of girl to take to the movies—when you want to see the picture.
- There goes a girl with polish—on her fingernails.
- Get a load of those legs. I've seen better looking bones in soup.
- There you have the greatest single argument for twin beds.
- She's just sore that I can read her like a book—and I like to read in bed.

With the male drunk, of course, or the male bore—laugh yourself well:

- He's thinking of quitting drinking. He's beginning to see the handwriting on the floor.
- This guy never has a hangover—he stays drunk.
- He only drinks on special occasions—like when somebody else is buying.
- Will you please follow the example of your head and come to a point?
- Please don't talk when I'm interrupting.

- He's not himself today—and it's a great improvement.
- You don't know what makes him tick—but you wish it were a time bomb.

THELMA LEE was heckled by a bore who yelled, "Hey, baby, take off your clothes." She squelched him with a line from *Kismet*: "Don't work up an appetite if you have no teeth."

Here are some favorite heckler squelches from the top comics:

- You're a real magician—you just made an ass of yourself.
- He's suffering from bottle fatigue.
- You know, I'm forming an attachment for you. It fits right over your mouth.
- I know this guy. He never opens his mouth unless he has nothing to say.

Most hecklers are easy to handle if you know what they are—and the types are easy to spot:

The Ego:

- Every time he opens his mouth he puts his feats into it.
- He's so conceited he has his X-rays retouched.

The Tightwad:

- If he went to the Last Supper, he would have tried to write it off.

The Dumb-Dumb:

- He's a man who really got it all together. Unfortunately, he forgot where he put it.
- The only thing that can stay in his head more than an hour is a cold.
- If he said what he thought, he'd be speechless.
- She has no more on her mind than anywhere else.

- Brains aren't everything. In fact, in her case they're nothing.

The Failures:
- He has risen from obscurity and is headed for oblivion.
- He has a fat chance to succeed—and a head to match.

Here are some answers that will fit any pain-in-the-audience:

- Let's play horse. I'll be the front end and you just be yourself.
- Why don't you take a long walk on a short pier?
- The next time you pass my house, I'll appreciate it.
- Do go away. I want to forget you exactly as you are.
- Please don't insist on telling me who you are. Let me detest you incognito.
- If I've said anything to insult you, believe me, I've tried my best.

5
A Dais in the Life of Everyone

Speeches are like babies—easy to conceive, but hard to deliver—unless you've done your homework. Anybody can make a speech if he's prepared for battle, and in this arena your weapons are words, jokes, and laughs. That's the reason for these notes. I'll supply the material and the examples, and tell you where and how to use them. But you'll have to practice by yourself. Even MILTON BERLE didn't have a good delivery when he was born—no matter what his mother told me.

Choose the joke or gag that fits you and the situation, and then repeat it to any friend that will listen. If you don't have a friend, buy a dog. Most men use their wives to try out their material. In some cases that helps them win an audience—but lose a wife (which may have been their idea in the first place).

The important thing is that the words, jokes, and laughs fit and fit you.

Once, when WILL ROGERS was criticized for using the word "ain't," he said, "Maybe 'ain't' ain't correct—but I notice a lot of folks who ain't usin' the word 'ain't' ain't eatin'." For him, that style was great, but for a WILLIAM BUCKLEY it would be inappropriate.

At one Catholic benefit for Cardinal Yo Pin I said, "I better not do any religious jokes today. The last time I did was six years ago, and I haven't won in bingo since." Sure it's funny, but I couldn't do the same line in talking about a DEAN MARTIN or a JACKIE GLEASON.

Politicians are sworn to take it. "I'm not really as good as you said, but I'm much better than you're thinking." At one dinner for SENATOR D'AMATO I started, "I've known some of the best politicians money could buy—not you, Senator." The double laugh satisfied the people *and* the Senator. At a function for CONGRESSMAN MARIO BIAGGI I noted, "The disadvantage of giving a politician a free hand is, he usually winds up putting it in your pocket—not you, Mario." Nobody laughed harder than Biaggi.

When REAGAN was campaigning against JIMMY CARTER for President, I introduced him at one fund-raiser. "I hope he becomes President—so I won't have to see him in pictures any more." Reagan said, "I can take a hint, but look at Carter. Three years ago he started out as Jimmy *who*? Now after three years he has become Jimmy *why*? Anyway, I don't want to say anything about Jimmy Carter's integrity, but a man who says he enjoys ice cold showers every morning will lie about other things too."

R. R. really laughed Carter out of office. I said to Reagan, "We don't have time for you. If President Carter isn't reelected, just think how much time the American people will have to waste learning to dislike somebody else." He answered, "Carter has been fooling the people long enough. How about giving me a chance?"

Every politician is rehearsed, even to say "hello." The average pol couldn't ad-lib a sneeze without help. I recall one candidate who was called on to make a speech: "I was so surprised in getting my nomination," he blurted out, "I almost dropped my acceptance speech."

One congressman faced a very warm audience one election eve.

"Now, before I start my speech," he said, "I woulc
something!"

A good politician is prepared for any and all emergenc
with the President when he arrived at a big fund-raising ...er.
He said to an aide, "Give me a list of all the people here who I
call by their first names."

Any comic worth his weight in smart-ass repartee has been
wearing out his files to meet any attack. Two of the great comics
of all time, FRED ALLEN and JACK BENNY, had a comedy feud on
radio that had dozens of their writers working overtime—and
they rehearsed pretty good.

One day, Fred and Jack met at the Friars' round table for lunch.
One pal suggested they continue their feud at the table. Allen
said to Benny, "Are they kidding? You couldn't ad-lib a belch
after a Hungarian dinner." Jack said, "Oh yeah? You wouldn't
say that if my writers were here!"

That's what I've been telling you. To be the life of the party,
Republican or Democratic, social, business, or sexual, you've
got to be ready. My portable gag file will prepare you, and your
preparation will insure you.

I was prepared when I introduced PHYLLIS DILLER at one party:
"How do you introduce a gal like Phyllis Diller? Just another
pretty face? They tell me she may be playmate of the month, but
who would want to? With her new figure she may go into
pictures. They want her for the MAE WEST parts. The only trouble
is her old parts don't work as good as Mae West's."

Of course, Phyllis was ready for me: "They say Joey has a lousy
personality. That's a lie. He has no personality at all. One thing
about this Adams guy—he speaks his mind. The trouble is, it
limits his conversation."

I was ready for WILLIAM BUCKLEY when I introduced him at a

conservative dinner: "Mr. Buckley is right of GENGHIS KHAN. What can I say about Buckley that hasn't been said about any fascist? I think Bill and his brother, SENATOR JIM, are the greatest brother act since the Jones Boys."

Bill Buckley said, "JOEY ADAMS has a pristine, ubiquitous, didactic attitude." Then to me, "I'll use words. Get somebody to explain them to you." Then to the audience, "Joey is so dumb he thinks high cholesterol is a religious holiday."

It all sounds like it's off the cuff, but those cuffs are prepared with the right gags for the right person at the right time.

GOVERNOR MARIO CUOMO and GOVERNOR HUGH CAREY were equipped with the gags from my venom file when they met in combat in the shark-infested gubernatorial race. "If he goes to Washington," Cuomo said, "Carey will double-cross the Potomac." Mario said, "Hugh is used to attending such dinners—in fact, he's the only one in the state to come to banquets like this with a food taster." Hugh was ready: "Cuomo is not a bad guy—until you get to know him."

I tell every politician to laugh the loudest when he is put down. But while you're laughing, remember to sharpen your own scalpel.

SENATOR D'AMATO rehearsed his ad libs about RONALD REAGAN. "He's a very religious man—he worships himself." I had Reagan's answer at the ready: "One thing about D'Amato—when he makes up his mind, he's full of indecision."

Mayor JOHN LINDSAY called me one day to tell me that he was speaking at a dinner where I was the toastmaster. He needed gags, "and get me on early so I do the jokes first." I gave the mayor some of my best one-liners. I studied the rest of the guests on the dais and gave him a line to fit each one. "BURT REYNOLDS is giving up his career to become an actor." "MICKEY ROONEY was a very small baby. When he was born his father handed out cigar butts." To DEAN MARTIN: "Go over to the brewery and have them put a head on you." "GEORGE BURNS is so old, he doesn't learn history—he remembers it." "A funny thing happened to SPIRO AGNEW last week. He opened his mouth and a foot fell out." "RODNEY DANGERFIELD went to a psychoanalyst for years, and it helped. Now he gets rejected by a much better class of girls." "LIBERACE is afraid of the dark. When he goes to sleep, he leaves his jacket lit." "WOODY ALLEN's hobby is to relax in a tub. He stays in it for hours. Sometimes he even fills it with water."

I not only gave JOHN LINDSAY all these gangs, but I rehearsed him—over the phone, at his apartment, and again in the men's room right before we all walked onto the dais.

Just as I started the festivities, an evil spirit struck me. I did every single joke that Lindsay had been rehearsing. I've got to admit I was hilarious, even if Lindsay didn't think so. For a moment I was a little sorry for the mayor—but then he turned it all around, and I was the guy they were sorry for.

He stepped grandly to the microphone and smiled. "I met JOEY ADAMS in the men's room right before we sat down," he said. "Poor Joey, he was distraught. He's a comic—that's his business—and he wanted to make good for you because you're a show business audience, and he didn't have a speech, so I gave him mine. You just heard it—so good night."

I must admit I did not prepare him for that line. But I also will admit that I put it in my mental computer to be used in an emergency; that is, when they do some of my gags before I go on—or when the comic or star is too tough to follow.

Of course, it doesn't matter if the joke is "old" or "new," only whether it's well chosen and well told. Even more important, it must be short and sharp. Please notice that all the gags I give you tell the whole story in one line.

e some loving putdowns you can use on the right target:

- He opened a halfway house for girls who couldn't go all the way.
- He never gives up. He's still holding an I.O.U. from Judge Crater.
- A priest should be allowed to get married and find out what hell really is.
- Our guest of honor is a humble and modest man—and with good reason.
- He has never been bored himself—but he *is* a carrier.
- He can get any girl he pleases. Up to now he hasn't pleased very many.
- You don't hear about the nice things he does. That's because he doesn't do nice things.
- He's in the same condition as the Great Wall of China—stoned.
- I have not known our guest of honor long, but I know him as long as I intend to.
- Our guest of honor is a man who, ever since he's been old enough to work, hasn't.
- To him a woman's body is a temple, and he tries to attend services as often as possible.
- Before his wife lets him in bed at night, he has to show his American Express Card.
- They say drinking interferes with your sex life, but with this guy it's the other way around.
- He's not too swift. He's the kind who would steal a car and keep up the payments.
- Nothing is impossible for the executive who doesn't have to do it himself.
- Dumb? It takes him an hour and a half to watch "Sixty Minutes."
- He goes with this girl, Sylvia. Everybody says she's a ten, but I happen to know she charges twenty.
- He willed his body to science and science contested the will.

- He went to college for four years and it cost him $50,000, when you add up all that beer.
- Our next speaker is well known. He's been written up many times. He's got ninety-eight parking tickets.
- He's the inventor of the do-it-yourself massage parlor.
- He gives a lot of money to the church. It's called, "Our Lady of the Tax Shelter."
- He has the body of an eighteen-year-old—waiting for him in the car.
- Some lover. The last time he had sex, his self-winding watch stopped.
- The only sex life he has is when his doctor tells him to cough.
- Our guest of honor has an unlisted phone, a numbered bank account, and a post office mailing address, which is all unnecessary because nobody really wants to reach him in the first place.

If you're playing for laughs, you've got to do these lines like you mean them. There is no sweet humor. When you insert the scalpel, you can't dull the edge by saying, "I'm only joking."

You can't say, "PHYLLIS DILLER has turned many a head in her day, and a few stomachs too," and then add, "but she's a nice girl." If she wasn't a nice girl and a friend, you wouldn't be there speaking for her or about her.

His EMINENCE CARDINAL COOKE always warned me to treat him like any other guest. He laughed the loudest when I said at one Catholic dinner, "About the pill, your Eminence, if you don't play the game, don't make the rules." But I said it with conviction, and that's why Cardinal Cooke led the laughter.

A good toastmaster or guest speaker will cool it by taking the heat himself. After one big build-up I said to the toastmaster, "Thank you. You said it exactly as I wrote it out for you."

WILL ROGERS invariably scratched his head in disbelief when he received one of those grand intros. "Thanks, you couldn't have been nicer to me if I died, or maybe you're anticipating my act."

STEVE ALLEN has his own way of loosening a tight halo. "It is always gratifying for a television entertainer to stand up in front of so many people who can't turn him off."

Wildly received at a fund-raising dinner in New York, JOHN F. KENNEDY quipped, "I'm deeply touched, but not as deeply touched as you have been by coming to this dinner."

BOB HOPE introduced me at a Boy Scout luncheon as one of the great personalities of radio. "I didn't exactly say it's a crime for you to get paid for doing what you do on the air. All I said was, you're the only radio performer I know who leaves the studio in a getaway car." I said, "Really? Well, you wouldn't say that if I were here in person. I really don't deserve this, but I have arthritis and I don't deserve that either." Then I really let him have it. "Anybody takes me for a fool makes no mistake. Listen, I know plenty. I just can't think of it."

My old pal GEORGIE JESSEL, called The Toastmaster General of the United States by four Presidents, always sounded like he just thought of the line. That was his trick. He'd scratch his head, or clear his throat, or puff on his cigar, and then throw the punch line. But the punch line was prepared long before he showed up at the dinner.

Georgie was the master at delivering eulogies, and they were always prepared. A lot of us refused to take his calls because we thought he was doing research. Jessel often delivered two or three eulogies in a day. At one particularly tender moment during a studied impassioned address, he accidentally glanced down at the man in the coffin. "My God," George gasped, "I *know* this man."

I introduced HENNY YOUNGMAN at one dinner and he was funny, with my material, of course, but he was on a little too long. "I'm sorry," he said, "that I stayed on longer than the allotted time, but I left my watch at home." I shouted up, "Don't you even have a pocket calendar?"

Even BOB HOPE has learned the lesson. At one dinner he was fine until the audience started to get restless. "This is terrible," he said, "I really don't know what to say." BERLE shouted, "You could say good-bye."

One speaker said about MAYOR KOCH of New York, "Personally, I'd like to see him run for President—anything to get him out of New York." How you gonna top that? Get the laugh and get the hell off.

BOB HOPE: "JOEY ADAMS received an honorary law degree at a Chinese University. I am told that a horse once graduated with an honorary degree from this institution. It was the first time in history a college gave an honorary degree to an entire horse."

Every one of these lines tells the story—a short story. WINSTON CHURCHILL's advice to speakers on a dais was, "Say what you have to say and the first time you come to a sentence with a grammatical ending, *sit down*."

Public speaking is like drilling for oil—if you don't strike oil in three minutes, stop boring! The first thing a good speaker should learn is that the Constitution guarantees free speech, but it doesn't guarantee listeners.

It's the same thing with humor. As soon as you hear that first big laugh—sit down. Make your speech as short as your prayers and you'll never be on too long.

You can't fool the people all the time. There's this politician who was explaining to the lady that he didn't go in for sports. "I got this tan making speeches—outdoors, in Florida." The woman heckled, "If you got so brown—you talked too much."

For years I have been supplying jokes, gags, and appropriate lines for dais speakers who have convinced me that money isn't everything. However, I love to do it to spread the laughter around.

That's the reason for this book. I don't want to share the wealth—just the laughs.

6
A First-Aid Kit of Humor

JIMMY DURANTE opened each show with, "You gotta start off each day wid a song." Well, if you can't sing, hum. If it's raining outside, use it for a laugh. "Just let a smile be your umbrella, and you'll get a mouthful of rain."

Thinking funny is a twenty-four-hour-a-day job. Did you have a bad night? Make a joke about it: "My insomnia is so bad I can't even sleep when it's time to get up." Hearing the laugh will heal you and it will help your listener as well. Remember what SINATRA said, "The only trouble with Italian coffee is that a week later you're sleepy again."

For "thinking funny" exercises, take your average day and pick out things that bug you, and turn them into a laugh. It's a sure cure for what ails you or the bugee.

Is your wife irritable? Laugh it off: "You promised to love, honor, and obey. Right now I'd settle for any one of them." Her laugh must make you both well. Is she overdrawn at the bank? Protect yourself with a good line: "The joint checking account is a device that permits the women to beat you to the draw."

Only your wife can louse up corn flakes? Save yourself by gagging. "The only thing she knows about good cooking is which restaurants serve it. . . . My wife is on a diet. That means *I* have to starve. The last time she went on a diet, *I* lost twelve pounds and $20,000 dollars. She bought a whole new wardrobe.

My wife prescribed, "No rich foods, no meats, no drinks. That should save you enough money to pay for my new gowns." She laughed me out of a fortune.

Is the stock market giving you a migraine that just split two for one? You've got to look at the positive side of Wall Street: "The sound, secure investments of today are the tax losses of tomorrow."

"You know you're getting older when it takes you longer to rest than to get tired," says BOB HOPE. "You know you're getting older," says RONALD REAGAN, "when you're faced with two temptations and you choose the one that gets you home by nine o'clock."

Laugh lines are better than age lines. You wake up in the morning and start to get dressed. You try to straighten out the wrinkles in your socks and discover you're not wearing any socks. Only a laugh line will help. JOLIE GABOR says, "If you can't afford to touch up your face, I'll show you how to touch up the date on your driver's license."

If you're alive and kicking, as all taxpayers are, reach for a gag before you start plea bargaining. "Remember, you need not file an income tax return if, as of December 31, 1983, you have been dead for a year or longer." "You can console yourself with the fact that the only people who don't mind getting flu shots are taxpayers—they're used to getting it in the end." "You can laugh at the fact that you never had it so good—nor had it taken away so fast by the IRS." "Don't blame the government for the tight money—just laugh at it." "They may not cure poverty, but the way they are raising taxes, they sure will cure wealth."

You go downstairs to get your car and find a parking ticket on it.

"I should have listened to my wife and bought a car without windshield wipers." I must remember to do what my friend SOUPY SALES did when he went to court with a parking ticket: "Plead insanity."

Traffic is terrible, and you may be late for your train—think of a gag, fast: "The shortest distance between two points is always under construction." You're standing still and the lady hits you with her 1950 Edsel. She says, "Why didn't you signal you were parked?" You may lose the train, but you won't lose your mind—or your sense of humor.

You drop into the Friars for lunch. It's a great day for you. You have a beautiful tan, your suit is custom-tailored, your head is high, and you are happy. You bump into HENNY YOUNGMAN, who looks at least twenty years older than you. His suit is wrinkled and so is his face. "JOEY ADAMS," he yells, "How did you let yourself get like that?" I've got to say, "I'm proud to be a friend of Henny Youngman—and it isn't easy being a man's only friend."

"It's good to see you," I said to Henny. "It means you're not behind my back." (If you want Henny's answers, go buy *his* book.)

You get into a taxi to go to the theater and you ask the cabbie, who just sits there, "Are you engaged?" He answers, "No, but I'm going steady." Then he wants to know where you're going, as he's just pulling in or going to lunch or can only go west or something. In other words, you've got to go where he wants to go. Now, you get out the real laugh artillery: "You're nobody's fool—but see if you can get somebody to adopt you!" If he's not laughing, change cabs or walk. Once I'd like to meet a taxi driver who would bawl you out for overtipping him.

The lunch tab is on the expense account but even then you don't want to pay the restaurant owner's rent for the year. Grab for a joke instead of the tab: "What's this ten dollars for on my bill?" "The chopped liver." "Whose liver was it, Rockefeller's?"

The boss is crying poverty. Laugh him out of it: "Running into debt isn't bad—it's running into creditors that hurts."

If the wife's charge accounts are really too much this month, show her your teeth in a smile instead of a sneer: "You'd make a hell of a congresswoman. You're always introducing new bills in the house." You'll get the laugh and she'll get the hint.

Many married men insist they are on speaking terms with their wives when all they do is listen. If you happen to be in that category, you can always have the last word—or the last laugh—without saying a thing. Don't talk in your sleep, just grin.

Don't let the weather get you down. Reach for a gag to pick you up.

- Is there a water shortage? Bathe with a friend.
- Is it too hot? KOCH is crazy for this weather. The potholes are melting.
- The politicians are the only ones who are happy in this weather. It's so humid, the money is sticking to them naturally.

SNOW?

- How about this weather? Do you realize this is the first snow job in weeks that hasn't come from Washington?
- Let's look at the bright side. The snow will fill up the potholes.

COLD?

- It was so cold in my room, every time I opened the door, the light went on.
- Our waterbed froze.
- It was so cold, LIZ TAYLOR decided to get married again.

- Well, at least you should have a warm air mass moving in from the northeast now that Congress is back in session.
- I got good news and bad news. My superintendent gave me the bad news. It's supposed to drop to five below zero tonight. The good news is he is finally going to fix my air conditioner.

STORMY WEATHER?

- You know, I wouldn't mind all this ice and sleet and snow and slush so much, if it only came in July when the weather is nice.

7
Adam's Rib

Every joke is about how *man* suffers: "Take my wife—*please.*" Or "One way for a husband to get the last word is to apologize." Or "I took my wife to the country, but she found her way back."

Now here's a chance for the women to strike back. DORIS DAY says "If it's true that men are such beasts, this must account for the fact that most women are animal lovers."

PRESIDENT REAGAN is for equal rights for women—all the way. Didn't he appoint a woman to the Supreme Court? Of course, she won't be paid as much as the guys.

I subscribe to the theory that women should never get married on a Sunday. It's just not right to gamble on a holy day.

A husband is a man who wishes he had as much fun when he's out as his wife *thinks* he has.

A liberated woman is one who has sex before marriage and a job after.

Famous sayings are often credited to the wrong people. I don't care who claims it. It was DOLLY PARTON who said, "It's what's up front that counts." And it wasn't WILL ROGERS, but ZSA ZSA, who said, "I never met a man I didn't like."

ANGIE DICKINSON says, "The trouble with most men is a woman marries one for life—and then discovers he doesn't have any."

A girdle is something like love. It binds us together and makes us better than we are by nature.

LIZ TAYLOR describes marriage: "Marriage is an agreement by which two people agree to be polite to each other in public."

The wife said, "If you do housework for $150 a week, that's domestic service. If you do it for nothing, that's matrimony."

Two women on the bus: "Tomorrow is my husband's birthday," one was saying. "What are you getting for him?" the other asked. "Make me an offer."

He said to her, "I love you terribly." She said, "You certainly do."

A smart girl doesn't trust a husband too far—or a bachelor too near.

I've seen a lot of smart guys with dumb women—but I never saw a smart woman with a dumb guy.

A man is only as old as he looks, and if he only looks—he's old.

I don't want to complain about my husband, but he just took a course in remedial sex.

She just got quick, quick relief from cold misery—a divorce.

Ever since I married, I never wake up grumpy. I let him sleep till noon.

Many couples break up because it looks like the marriage is going to last forever.

Women who want to be the equal of men lack ambition.

It's true money can't buy love, but it makes shopping more fun.

NANCY REAGAN sums it up. "Marriage is a lot like the U.S. constitution. A man begins by laying down the law to his wife—and ends by accepting all her amendments."

8
Special Occasion Pick-Me-Ups

If you want to remember your family or friends on a special day, send a smile or a laugh instead of a tear. It's cheaper than a present and will do much more good. And look at all the money you're saving. That should give *you* a good laugh.

HAPPY BIRTHDAY

- Aren't you glad to be at an age where the battle of the sexes is no longer your affair?
- The best thing about getting old is that all those things you couldn't have when you were young, you no longer want.
- When people tell you how young you look, they're telling you how old you are.
- Happy Birthday from my heart. Or would you prefer another part?
- I was tempted to buy you a real expensive present for your birthday. Congratulate me on my willpower.
- Happy Birthday, darling. I'll always remember your birthday, but never your age.

You're never sure how good a marriage is, so, if there's an *anniversary* coming up (even if it's your own), you're sure to make it a happy one if you send a laugh.

HAPPY ANNIVERSARY

- Living together is such a vogue now, many married couples keep their wedding a secret so they won't appear old-fashioned.
- A lot of people are living together who aren't married. And a lot of people are married who aren't living together.
- Congratulations! Marriage is like a friendship that somehow got out of control.
- Be kind to the lady you're married to. The wife you save may be your own.
- I'm glad you made it. Marriage is a gamble. Marry for love and you divorce for money; marry for money and you divorce for love. You gambled and won. Congratulations!

Start the *New Year* off right with a happy card.

HAPPY NEW YEAR

- Your car has just depreciated $2,000 and your wife's clothes are now last year's.
- May all your troubles last as long as your New Year's resolutions.
- Disliking people requires a reason. Loving doesn't. So, may I wish you a happy new year of love.

Valentine's Day should bring out the smile as well as the love. They go together.

BE MY VALENTINE

- It is better to have loved and lost—much better. Now I have *you.*
- Every day is Valentine's Day for me. I keep waiting for the perfect woman to come along. Meanwhile, I'm having fun with the imperfect ones.

- It's the time for lovers. To err is human, but it feels divine.
- I love you as no one has ever loved you before. And don't tell me you can't tell the difference.
- We're in the middle of a sexual revolution—let's get wounded.
- All the world loves a lover—except the husband.
- Would you ever think when Bing Crosby introduced "Love Thy Neighbor" it would cause all that wife-swapping all over Long Island?
- Love makes the world go 'round. How about going a few rounds with me?

MERRY CHRISTMAS

- Santa has the right idea. Visit people once a year and you'll always be welcome.
- It is better to give than to receive—especially if it's deductible.
- I'm giving money for Christmas presents this year. It's the cheapest thing I could find.

ALL-OCCASION LAUGH NOTES

Millions of notes are sent out every day. Some serious, some reminders, some important, some vital. Whatever the message, it will be easier to take if a laugh comes with it:

- Enjoy the sex act before Congress repeals it.
- If you can't give up sex, get married and taper off.
- Make someone happy today. Mind your own business.
- Diets are for people who are thick and tired of it.
- Join the campaign to end poverty. Send money.
- Sex is good for you, and you don't need batteries.
- The three favorite things in life are a martini before and a nap after.

- You know you're getting old when you go to a drive-in movie and keep the seat belt fastened.
- The trouble with business today is, when you're rich it's on paper; when you're poor, it's cash.
- Don't trust anything he says while he's in love, drunk, or running for office.
- Do it tomorrow. You made enough mistakes today.
- To play the market, you can be a bull or a bear, but you can't be chicken.
- Dieting is when you stop eating food and start eating calories.
- Eat, drink, and be merry—for tomorrow they may cancel your credit cards.
- To make a fortune, come up with something that is low priced, habit forming, and tax deductible.
- Money can't buy love, but it makes shopping more fun.
- To hell with the whales. Let's save the dollar.
- Help preserve wild life. Throw a party tonight.
- You can't take sex with you, so wear it out before you go.
- Never make love when you have something better to do. But what's better?
- Go on a diet now. The world is in bad shape—must you be too?
- If at first you don't succeed, try, try again. Then quit. It's no use making a damn fool of yourself.
- Jogging is good for you. More people are collapsing in perfect health than ever before.
- A well-balanced sex life is impossible in a canoe.
- We have the highest standard of living in the world. If only we could afford it.
- The chief cause of divorce is marriage.
- Question: Do you know what good clean fun is?
  Answer: No, what good is it?
- Credit cards have made buying easier, but paying harder.
- Marriage is the only cure for love.
- Do it now. There may be a law against it tomorrow.
- They say that people who are disappointed in love are compulsive eaters. So how come there are so many fat sultans?

- To err is human. To blame it on the other guy is politics.
- There's only one way to handle a woman. But nobody knows what it is.
- The best things in life are free. No wonder they are never advertised.
- If you want to know how to run a big business, ask a man who hasn't any.
- Save your money. Some day it may be worth something.
- Advice to loveworn: When wine, women, and song become too much for you, give up singing.
- A smart diplomat never stands between a dog and a lamp post.
- Marriage is wonderful. Without it husbands and wives would have to fight with perfect strangers.
- Marriage is great. It's the living together that's tough.
- Give a woman an inch, and immediately the whole family is on a diet.
- A genius is one who can do anything but make a living.
- There are two sides to every question—and a good politician takes both.
- A word to the wide is sufficient: If you cheat on a diet, you gain in the end.
- Eat, drink, and be merry—for tomorrow ye diet.
- It's tough to win. If you do something wrong, you're fined. If
- you do something right, you're taxed.
- To find the secret of your youth, lie about your age.
- Be kind to your friends. If it weren't for them, you'd be a total stranger.
- Candy is dandy, but sex doesn't rot your teeth.
- Cure virginity.
- Chastity is its own punishment.
- Support free enterprise—legalize prostitution.
- Save water. Bathe with friends.
- Don't marry for money. You can borrow it cheaper.
- There are more things in life than money. There are also credit cards and overdrafts.
- People who think they know everything always annoy those of us who do.

- Better late than audited.
- Two heads are better than one ass.
- If at first you don't succeed, failure may be your thing.
- Life insurance is what keeps a man poor all his life so he can die rich.

Use a gag for every occasion. You'll find jokes, gags, and anecdotes in the following gag file.

PART II

The Emergency Gag File—Yours for Adoption

Here come the jokes. There is no such thing as an old joke. If you never heard it before, it's new. Pick out the ones that fit the occasion, the party, the roast, the guest of honor, or the setting, and then try them out—even if your audience is only a mirror. Then when you're called on, hit the line hard! With confidence! A good joke or story or gag will never die if it's told right and if it fits. After all, where would BEETHOVEN and BACH be if you only played their music once? IRVING BERLIN or GEORGE GERSHWIN would have starved if you turned off the TV and radio every time their tunes came on, just because you heard them before.

There's the old gag about comics sitting around the table at the Friars Club, all throwing numbers at each other from the joke files. "Twenty-three," said BERLE, and everybody laughed. "Sixteen," said HOPE, and the others screamed. "Thirty-four" said BURNS, and they banged the table. I said, "Sixty-five" and nobody even smiled. "That's a good joke!" I yelled, "Why didn't you laugh?" BERLE said, "I don't like the way you tell it."

And don't worry about who these gags belong to. I specialize in retailing humor that I bought wholesale—or stole retail. So here is your personal gag file, with jokes, stories, and anecdotes looking for a home. With these tools you can meet any emergency. All you have to do is work the dictionary for the joke, story, line, or insult, from A for Age to Z for Zsa Zsa.

If you're looking to do a routine on ecology, look up P for Pollution. Or P for Politicians, or M for Mother-in-Law. There are heckle lines. Look under I for Insults, or S for Squelch. If you are on a political kick—look to D for Democrats, R for Republicans, or C for Crooks. If you want to talk about an honest politician, look up P for Psychiatrist, or C for Cemetery.

If you're talking about a conservative, look up R for Retarded. If it's the left you are interested in, look up C for Communist or C for China or R for Russia.

If you come home late for dinner, you can pick your excuse from many categories: O for Office or C for Cheating or T for Traffic or D for Drinking.

We have ethnic jokes and religious stories—from the Bible to the Borscht Belt. Look under I for Italy or J for Jewish or C for Church or Christian Science or B for Bible. You'll find black humor and Irish humor, Polish, Puerto Rican, and Scotch humor, all looking to be adopted by some nice family.

If you want lines about Texas, look up M for Money or B for Big or E for Exaggerate. If it's rich you're after, you'll find it under R for Rockefeller, M for Money, T for Texas or Taxes, or I for Inflation.

There are stories about sex or Boy Scouts, booze and broads, or boozed-up broads.

If you need happy jokes, look in the index under B for Bachelor or P for Prostitution. You will find Berle, Hope, and Youngman—old friends, with jokes to match. We also have the wit of GEORGE BERNARD SHAW, WILL ROGERS, and FRED ALLEN, which BERLE, HOPE, and YOUNGMAN are still using.

Here is a lifetime of research that I give to you. Use it with my blessing. The gags belong to you, now. If you steal one joke, it's plagiarism. If you steal a lot of jokes, it's research. I did all the research for you, so be my guest.

If you use all these gags—from A to Z—I do not promise you'll be the greatest thing since WILL ROGERS or even HENNY YOUNGMAN, but you will know the alphabet better. On the other hand, if you are a big hit, let me know and I'll try them myself.

Joey Adams Gag File Dictionary

Abortion

- The lady pest heckled the politician, "What are you going to do about abortion?" He answered, "Lady, in your case I'd be prepared to make it retroactive."
- The Reagan administration is still against abortion. They'll do anything to get another taxpayer.

Absent-minded

- The absent-minded guy took his car out for a walk and left his girl in the garage to be washed and lubricated.

Accountant

- The accountant's daughter lost her tooth. She put it under her pillow and asked the tooth fairy to leave a receipt for tax purposes.

Acquaintance

- Somebody we know well enough to borrow from but not well enough to lend to.

Acting

- KATHARINE HEPBURN says, "Acting is a minor gift and not a very high-class way to earn a living. After all, SHIRLEY TEMPLE could do it at the age of four."

Actor

- An actor is a guy who, if you ain't talking about him, he ain't listening.
- I love actors. I love them for their belief in God and themselves. And I hope they forgive me for giving God top billing.
- Some of the greatest love affairs I've known have involved one actor—unassisted.
- You can't put an actor down. I asked one star about his play that lasted one night. He said, "Oh the show was a great success, but the audience was a failure."
- One ham burst into the psychiatrist's office and shouted, "Doc! You've got to help me. I'm developing an inferiority complex." The shrink said, "Tell me about it." The star said, "It's awful. I'm beginning to think other people are just as good as I am."
- An actor showed up at one party with a deep tan. "Say," his hostess gushed, "What a sunburn, such a bronze. Where did you get it?" The star growled, "I have a lousy agent."

Actress

- She was willing to do anything to get in pictures. She finally made bad.

Adam and Eve

- As Adam said to Eve, "I wear the plants in this family."

Advertising

- Advertising people can make people live beyond their means —but so can marriage.

Advice

- It's always nicer to give than to receive, especially when you're talking about advice.
- The best time to give advice to your children is while they're still young enough to believe you know what you're talking about.

- Zsa Zsa says, "Fellows don't whistle at a girl's brains." Her theory is that "girls who do right get left."
- Advice to politicians: Always be sincere, whether you mean it or not.

Age

- Two male senior citizens were sitting on a park bench. An older lady thought she'd give them a thrill, undressed herself, and ran naked right in front of them. One fella said to the other, "What was that?" The other social security boy said, "I don't know, but whatever it was, it needed pressing."
- An eighty-year-old gentleman married a teenager. For a wedding present he gave her a do-it-yourself kit. I asked why he married her. He explained, "I decided it would be better to smell perfume for the remainder of my life than to smell liniment."
- The irony of life is that by the time you have money to burn, the fire has gone out.
- Most women don't really need doctors. They could add years to their lives if they would just tell the truth about their ages.
- I have an aunt who married so late in life that Medicare picked up eighty percent of the honeymoon.
- You're getting older when your dreams about girls are reruns.
- An eighty-year-old grandma walked a mile to the village library to reserve a copy of the latest sexy book. The librarian said, "I thought you only read history." The old gal answered, "At my age, this is history!"
- The condition of a man can best be judged by what he takes two at a time—stairs or pills.
- You know you're getting older when the little old lady you're helping across the street is your wife.
- CHARLES DARWIN, famous for his theory of evolution, was 172 years old in February. REAGAN says, "I didn't agree with his theory and spent many nights trying to talk him out of the whole thing."
- One thing I don't like about PRESIDENT REAGAN. I wish he'd

stop referring to everybody under sixty-five as "junior citizens."

- PHYLLIS DILLER complained to me, "They sure aren't making mirrors the way they use to. The ones I buy now are full of wrinkles!"

Airlines

- There's definitely an advantage to flying first class. You get where you're going eighteen feet sooner than people in coach.
- They're raising flying rates daily. A friend of mine flew to New York first class and arrived there tourist.
- HELEN KARDON figures with so many airlines in financial trouble, the only folks making money at our airports these days are the Hare Krishnas.
- The kids were trying to talk Grandma into taking her first plane trip. "Not me," she said, "I don't go for those newfangled things. I'm gonna sit right here and enjoy my television like the Lord intended."

Airport

- That's a place people go to find out how late their flight is going to be.

Alibi

- The judge told the man, "You are accused by your landlord of being drunk and setting fire to the bed." He alibied, "It's a lie. The bed was on fire when I got into it."

Alimony

- My aunt told me, "My first husband wants to marry me again, but I suspect he's after the money I married him for."
- My neighbor's wife keeps reminding him that her allowance isn't as big as her alimony will be.

- The problem with paying alimony is that it's like pumping gas into another man's car.
- A splitting headache.
- The fee a woman charges for name dropping.

America
- Every child born in America is endowed with life, liberty, and a share of the national debt.

American
- An American is not afraid to tell off the President of the United States, but he's very polite to a meter maid.

American
- A politician who is given a job abroad in order to get him out of the country.

American Express
- HENNY YOUNGMAN says, "I call my wife American Express. She always says, "Don't leave home without me."

Animals
- AUDREY HEPBURN notes, "Some women think men are animals and maybe they're right. A man can be as meek as a lamb, brave as a tiger, and have the courage of a lion. But the minute he meets a pretty girl, he becomes a jackass."
- The butterfly asked the hummingbird why he hums. "Because I don't know the words."

Anonymous
- CHARLES ALFIERI tells about the oddball who used an alias, had an unlisted phone number, and a Swiss bank account. When he died, they couldn't find him to bury him.

Antique
- An antique is a piece of modern furniture which is old by the time you get through making the payments.

- An antique is an object that has made a round trip to the attic.

Apartment
- A home that is sometimes heated by oil, sometimes by electricity, but more often by complaining to the superintendent.
- There are three kinds of apartment buildings in New York today. They're either going *up*, coming *down*, or *fully rented.*
- I told the manager of my building the apartment had roaches. He raised my rent for keeping pets.

Apartment Building
- A place where the landlord and the tenant are both trying to raise the rent.

Arabs
- I really don't know if the Arabs are taking over, but my bank tellers are wearing turbans.

Army
- RIP TAYLOR claims he hated the Army. "If I wanted little sleep and lousy food, I would have just moved in with my wife's folks."
- The Army was a real learning experience for me. I learned I wanted to be a civilian.
- BILL MURRAY is the one who said it: "Drafting women makes a lot of sense. If we have a war and the women fight and we win, that's O.K., and if we lose we can say, 'Big deal, you beat a bunch of girls.'"

Art
- I remember the time I was thrown out of my art class in school. They were drawing live nudes and I tried to trace one.
- JAN MURRAY says, "Last week I spent 3 hours painting the girl next door in the nude. Then my wife came around and made me put on a robe."

Art Theater
- That's where the theater is clean, but the pictures are filthy.

Artist

- This character approached a lady and said, "I'd like to capture you on canvas." She said, "You mean you want to paint my portrait?" He said "No, I've got an Army cot in the back of my camper."

Astrologist

- My neighbor asked his astrologist if it's unlucky to postpone a wedding. He said, "Not if you keep postponing it."

Atheist

- Suitable epitaph for tombstone of an atheist: "Here lies an atheist, all dressed up and nowhere to go."
- I finally discovered the true meaning of the word "atheist." It's a teenager who doesn't believe in rock and roll.
- Overheard between two goldfish: "Okay wise guy, if there is no God, just answer me one question. Who changes the water every day?"

AT&T

- The telephone company made a $6 billion profit last year, which proves one thing. While we were reaching out to touch someone, they were putting the touch on us.

Automation

- With the increasing respect for computerized judgment we will soon accept the personality evaluation on weight machines as character references.

Availability

- Most girls find that the one quality they admire most in men is availability.

Babies

- Babies start bawling the moment they are born. In the first place, they're hungry. In the second place, by the time they're five minutes old, they owe the IRS $2,500.

Bachelor

- A man who prefers to cook his own goose.
- WARREN BEATTY describes a bachelor as someone who occasionally wonders who would make the best wife—a blonde, brunette, or redhead. But he always comes to his senses in the end and remembers that it really doesn't matter what color the truck is if it's gonna run him over anyway.
- A man who believes that one can live as cheaply as two.
- If a man has both a savings account and a checking account, the chances are he's a bachelor.
- My neighbor says he feels sorry for bachelors. What do they do for aggravation?

Bad Luck

- While the bank robber was inside, the finance company repossessed the getaway car.

Bankrupt

- I consoled Mrs. Richards, "I just heard about your poor husband going bankrupt. I feel so sorry for him." She sighed, "So do I. He's going to miss me so."
- The big business tycoon was asked why he wants to go bankrupt. He said, "I hate to owe money."

Banks

- What we need in this country is a bank where you deposit a toaster and they give you money.
- A place that holds your money so inflation can eat it.

Bar Mitzvah

- My nephew did a switch. He sent his father a $1,000 check for his bar mitzvah. The old man signed it and sent it back.

Bargain

- It takes two to make a bargain—but one to get stuck.
- A bargain is something you can't use at a price you can't resist.
- Anything you can buy for only twice what it's worth.

Baseball

- There is only one trouble with baseball. The guy who can pitch, bat, field, and run bases better than anybody else on the team is usually sitting in the bleachers.
- I must admit baseball is still the national sport. Now go and convince ELIZABETH TAYLOR and ZSA ZSA.

Beggar

- The bum asked the man for a dollar. "If you would ask for a dime or a quarter you could have a better chance of making money," the man advised. The bum said, "Give me what you want, but don't tell me how to run my business."
- He's not afraid of work. He fought it for years, and won.

Belief

- Your friends don't believe you make as much as you say you do, and the government doesn't believe you make as little.

Beverly Hills

- Beverly Hills is so exclusive, it's the only town in America where Chicken Delight has an unlisted number.
- I've seen snobs. They are so chic in Beverly Hills they wear contact sunglasses.

Bible

- I'm the guy that didn't object to the *Reader's Digest* coming out with a condensed version of the Bible, although I was a bit surprised that in the story of Noah, instead of raining forty days and forty nights, the short version says it rained all weekend.
- I did like the new version of Adam and Eve where it says they had to leave the Garden of Eden because it was going condo.
- Now the story is out that God called his writers together. "Gentlemen, I have a big show on Mt. Sinai and I need some material." One volunteered, "How about Thou shalt not steal?" Another suggested, "Thou shalt not kill." A third said said, "Thou shall not . . ." God interrupted, "Wait. How many times have I told you I can't use one-liners."

• MILTON BERLE explains why the Bible tells us that the first man, Adam, lived in Paradise. "It helps if you remember he had no mother-in-law."

Bigamist

• DR. JOYCE BROTHERS says, "These days a man supporting two wives is not necessarily a bigamist. His son may have gotten married."

Bikini

• What they reveal is suggestive. What they conceal is vital.

Bilious

• The nauseous feeling you get when you open your mail the first of the month.

Bills

• She couldn't pay the grocer. She had given all she had to the butcher. The kid said, "Mama, the bill collector is here. Have you got the money or do you want me to go out and play for awhile?"

Birth Control

• HENNY YOUNGMAN says, "I just discovered a new birth control device. My wife takes off her makeup."
• I know a woman who took aspirin instead of birth control pills. Nine months later she had a baby who never gets a headache.

Boomerang

• What do you call a boomerang that won't come back? A stick.

Bore

• A person who has nothing to say—and says it.
• One who insists upon talking about himself when you want to talk about yourself.

Borscht Belt

- The Borscht Belt has gotten so big, they are thinking of air-conditioning an indoor mountain and having tiger hunting under glass.

Bosses

- Today we take up the plight of the bosses. A businessman can't win nowadays. If he does something wrong, he's fined; if he does something right, he's taxed.
- If you want to know how to run a business, ask a man who hasn't any.
- One manufacturer cried to me, "Business is so bad, even the people who don't intend to pay aren't buying."
- The applicant agreed the job sounded okay but he told the boss the last place he worked paid more. The future employer asked. "Did they give you rest periods, life insurance, and vacations with pay?" He said "Yes, and a $1,000 holiday bonus and all holidays off." The boss asked, "Then why did you leave?" He said, "The company went bankrupt."
- "This is just a suggestion. You don't have to follow it unless you want to keep your job."

Brevity

- A debtor on the witness stand cried, "As God is my judge, I do not owe the money." Judge replied, "He is not. I am. You do."
- The quality that makes speeches, politicians, and sex bearable.

Budget

- "I really don't want a lot of money," my neighbor's wife explained. "I just wish we could afford to live the way we're living now."
- You figured your budget perfectly, if the money you owe is the same amount you spent.
- My neighbor's definition of a budget is a family quarrel.

- An orderly system for a living beyond your means.
- I finally figured out the reason why household budgets never seem to work. It's because the husband works only five days a week while the wife spends seven days a week.
- Washington bureaucrats have finally figured out how to balance the budget. They're going to tilt the country.
- The woman struggling with a pile of bills said to her husband, "The only fair thing is to flip a coin. Heads I spend less, tails you earn more."

Buried at Sea

- JOHN ROCHE asks, "Did you hear about the admiral who was buried at sea? Four of his friends were drowned digging the grave."

Buses

- One woman missed her bus the other day and started hollering. The cop said encouragingly, "If you run you can catch it." She said, "If I run I can beat it."

George Bush

- Vice President Bush took the public tour through the White House because he wanted to see it at least once.

Business

- The dress manufacturer received a wire from a customer saying, "Cancel order at once." The reply: "Regret your order cannot be canceled at once. You will have to wait your turn."
- The head of the brokerage house gave this pep talk to his staff: "One day, as I sat musing, sad and lonely and friendless, a kindly voice came to me from out of the gloom saying, 'Cheer up, things could be worse.' And so, gentlemen, I cheered up... and sure enough, they got worse."
- He's doing very well in the business world. He had two fires and he only needed one of them.

- I asked the boss why he bargains about prices when he's buying merchandise. "I happen to know you're going into bankruptcy." He said, "I don't want to owe too much."
- The manufacturer sent the merchant a letter telling him he could not fill his order until the previous order was paid for. The merchant wired him, "Please cancel order—can't wait that long."
- PUDGY spotted a sign of the economic times in midtown Manhattan the other day when she passed a little dress shop that displayed a window placard reading, "Business as usual—crucial!"
- My son is a good businessman," Mrs. Adler said proudly. "He's so dedicated that he keeps his secretary near his bed in case he should get an idea during the night."
- "How can you make money selling watches so cheap?" "Easy. We make our profit repairing them."

Busybodies

- That's what they call prostitutes in Australia.

California

- BOB HOPE says he likes the California sunshine. "Every once in a while we get novelty weather, like rain. After a really big rain, you can see CHARLTON HESTON on the freeway parting the waters."

Cannibal

- A cannibal rushed into his village to spread the word that a hunting party had captured a politician. "Good," said one of the cannibals enthusiastically, "I've always wanted to try a baloney sandwich."
- LORETTA LOHR tells about the cannibal cook who asked the chief, "Shall I boil this missionary?" He said, "No, stupid, this one is a friar."

- A cannibal's thought while passing a cemetery: All that good food gone to waste.
- Cannibal husband to wife: "How many people for dinner tonight?" Wife to husband: "Just one, dear."
- Did you hear about the cannibal who ate his mother-in-law and then discovered that she still disagreed with him?

Careful

- "I want a very careful man," the lady told the plumber. "I want a man who will take no risks of any kind." He said, "I'm your man, lady. May I have my fee in advance?"

Car Insurance

- I got a great auto insurance company. My policy comes with a $100 debatable.

Cars

- The garage mechanic said to the car owner, "My advice is to keep the oil and change the car."
- WARREN BEATTY bought a new, expensive car: "You'll love it. It gets more gals to the mile."
- Maybe we should go back to the big luxury cars. These little economy cars are too expensive.
- In the house with teenagers, the only time father gets to use the car is when he has to drive downtown to pay an installment on it.
- They keep talking about crime in the streets. To me that's the price of new cars.
- My neighbor told me, "I paid $16,000 for a new car but it gets me where I'm going—the welfare office."
- Nowadays if you want to by a $10,000 car, it's easy. Buy a $3,000 car on time.
- A VW breaks down. A Rolls Royce malfunctions.
- It could only happen in Detroit. They are making cars smaller without cutting the size of the prices.

Carter

- Poor Jimmy. He left the government in such bad financial shape, when he got his first pension check it bounced.

Cats

- Once upon a time there were two cats prowling a back fence. "Meow," said one. The other said, "Moo." The first said, "What do you mean, 'Moo'?" The second said, "I'm studying a foreign language."

Celebrity

- HENRY KISSINGER says, "The nice thing about being a celebrity is that when you bore people they think it's their fault."

Census

- The census-taker discovered there was no job classification on the census form for the oldest profession, so he entered the lady concerned as a mattress worker.

Central Park

- STEVE KESSLER passed by Central Park last night and reports, "I saw four people jogging and three people running for their lives."

Chaperones

- People who couldn't make the team but went along to intercept the passes.

Chaplain of the Senate

- Does not pray for the Senate. He watches the Senate—and prays for the country.

Charity

- As the minister said, "Let's give freely and generously of our income—as reported to the IRS."

Cheap

- Cheap? He's the only guy I know who walks off airplanes carrying a doggie bag.
- He's really cheap. He's mad because he got well before his pills gave out.
- He works for the government as a dollar-a-year man, and even out of that he manages to save a little.

- He asked his wife if she would go to the opening of the new show without a new gown. She said, "Absolutely not." He said, "That's what I figured—so I only bought one ticket."

Cheap Rate

- There's a new cheap-rate service to Australia now. But some pending passengers get worried when they see the notice: "Please note that all lifeboats are reserved for the 'Go now, pay later' passengers."

Cheating

- There's one hotel in town that's strictly for cheaters. In fact, when a couple registers, they sign in as Mr. and Mrs. To-Whom-It-May-Concern. One guy followed his wife there and he broke into the room and found her making love to his best friend. "You'll pay for this," he shouted. The friend said calmly, "Are you on American Express? I never leave home without it."
- Two doctors talking: "I know you've been making love to my wife. What do you think of her?" The second doctor says, "Don't you know?" The first says, "Yes, but I wanted a second opinion."
- My neighbor confided in me, "I told my wife the truth. I told her I was seeing a psychiatrist. And she told me the truth. She is seeing a psychiatrist, two plumbers, and a bartender."
- "Your honor," she told the judge, "I want a divorce. My husband has been cheating on me. Just last night I was walking down Broadway when I saw him go into a movie with another woman." "Then why didn't you follow them into the theater to find out who she was. It may have been just a harmless coincidence. You should have gone in after them." "I would have, but the fellow I was with had already seen the picture."
- A good man is hard to find—until the husband opens the closet door.
- My neighbor saw this guy in front of his house jogging naked. "How come you're jogging without any clothes on?" he asked him. His answer was, "Because you came home early."

- An eighty-year-old gentleman went to the hospital for his annual checkup. The doctor examined him and said, "You won't live another week if you keep chasing women." The old boy said, "Don't be ridiculous, I'm healthy as a bull." "I know, the doctor said, "one of the women is my wife!"
- I am firmly against husbands and wives cheating. I am firmly against anything I can't do.
- You know, there really is such a thing as a happily married couple. It's any husband who's going out with another man's wife.
- My neighbor told me, "I was married once. Now I just lease."
- My friend told me, "When I met my wife she didn't have a social life. In fact, she didn't start dating until after we were married."
- I said, "I hear you caught your husband cheating and you had a terrible argument." She said, "Oh, I wouldn't say that. It's true we had a fight and I stabbed him, but that's as far as it went."
- My neighbor says, "I know I'll sound old-fashioned, but I just don't believe in trial marriages. I think they're very dangerous. If you're not careful they can lead to the real thing."
- He said, "We almost did get married. Two days before the wedding we had this big fight about going out with the guys to an all-night stag party. Finally I said if it meant that much to her, she could go ahead and do it."
- I don't know who said it. I think it was me. "Every man cheats—and he is only honest when he's discovered."

Childbirth

- The unwed mother was in the hospital nursing her illegitimate child, when the doctor entered. "Your hair is red," said the doctor, "but the child's hair is brown. What was the color of the father's hair?" The mother said, "I really don't know—he didn't take his hat off."

Children

- What we need nowadays is a child labor law—to keep children from working their parents to death.

- The only way to let your kids know you're home is to walk in front of the TV set.
- Insanity is hereditary. You get it from your children.
- My uncle always said, "Lucky are the mothers and fathers who have no children."
- SAL LORE, JR., says, "I had a very strange childhood. My mother was so naive. One time she read the label on an aspirin bottle that said, 'Keep away from children'—and I haven't seen her since."

China
- You can say anything you please—but only once.
- Would you believe that sex is finding its place in China? I opened a fortune cookie that came with a foldout.

Chinese
- Do you know that there are 800 million Chinese? I know they read the teachings of Lenin, but some of them must be sneaking a look at Masters and Johnson.

Christmas
- My neighbor sends out Christmas cards without signing them. He says he wants to spread season's greetings—but he doesn't want to get involved.
- From under the tree my wife hollered, "Here's your most beautiful present." I said, "I'd love to see it." She said, "Wait a minute and I'll put it on."
- I saved my wife a lot of standing in line this Christmas. I didn't give her a present. I gave her an exchange certificate. Who needs a middleman?
- I hope you had a Christmas you'll never forget, and a New Year's you can't remember.

Church
- There's a sign in front of the church in Cleveland that says, "Come in for a faith lift."

Chutzpah

- One bum approached me and said, "I know, I know, I owe you $300." I said, "It's only $200." He said, "It's gonna be $300."
- Chutzpah is super nerve. It's when you make an obscene phone call collect.
- Chutzpah is a guy who goes to the bank for a loan and says, "I only want enough money for a one-way ticket to Europe."

Cigarettes

- The government puts health warnings on packages of cigarettes. Why don't they put them on bombs?

Circus

- The new sword swallower was demonstrating his act for me backstage by swallowing some pins and needles. He explained, "I'm on a diet."

Class

- That RODNEY DANGERFIELD has it. He arrived formally attired at WOLFE's Sixth Avenue deli wearing his soup and fish—all over his vest.

Class Reunion

- A class reunion is the same old faces with more new teeth.

Clean

- PHYLLIS DILLER says, "My mother was a cleanliness nut. At the table she used to tie a pigeon to my neck so there wouldn't be any crumbs."

Cocktail Party

- A good cocktail party can be deflating. At one book-warming this gushing fan collared the bewildered author to tell him, "I read your book as a serial in the *New York Post,* in the book form, and as a condensation, and now I've seen it in the movies and on TV. Frankly, Mr. Imglick, just what the hell are you trying to say?"

Cold

- J. LOMANDKI suggests it was so cold that BROOKE SHIELDS let a pair of long johns come between her and her Calvins.
- It was so cold on Eighth Avenue that the prostitutes couldn't wait for the cops to pull them in.
- It was so cold my teeth were chattering—and they were in a glass next to my bed.
- ROCHELLE SMITH says, "It was so cold I stayed home and my eyes froze on Joey Adams's column."
- It was so cold my lawyer had his hands in his own pocket.
- It was so cold we would have welcomed a hot foot.
- It was so cold, my watch rubbed its hands together.

College

- Colleges now have co-ed dorms. I've heard of room service, but this is ridiculous.

Comedian

- A fellow who knows a good joke when he steals one.

Communism

- In Russia there is freedom of speech. But there is no guarantee of freedom after speech.
- A famous athlete who recently escaped from behind the Iron Curtain was running. He said, "We use the border for the finish line."

Community Property

- I realize a wife is entitled to half of everything—but not in advance!

Compensation

- It takes people a long time to get over an illness if compensation sets in.

Compliment

- BOB HOPE sent this compliment on my column: "You have a fertile mind, and you know what makes things fertile."

Computers

- The husband came home exhausted. "What a day I had—the computer broke down and I had to think."
- A little old lady walked into the credit department at American Express and demanded, "I don't care to bandy words with underlings about my overdue account. Take me to your computer."
- JEAN STAPLETON said, "Someday, we are told, the machine will take over the world. That's why I always talk very politely on the telephone when a recording answers."

Congress

- Some men join the navy and see the world. Others just join Congress.
- ERNEST BORGNINE says, "I don't understand why they say congressmen spend money like drunken sailors. Sailors spend their own money!"
- It is the first nut house I've ever known that's run by the inmates.
- If we play "Hail to the Chief" when the President makes an entrance, why can't Congress have its own song when it convenes: "Send in the Clowns."
- Where a man gets up to speak, says nothing, nobody listens, and everybody disagrees.

Conservative

- A conservative goes to a nudie movie for the message—or to a French picture and reads the titles.

Considerate

- Holding the door for your wife while she carries a load of groceries.

Consultant

- A man who knows 101 ways to make love—but doesn't know any women.

Convict

- One convict was telling his cellmate, "It all went to wine, women, and lawyers."

Cooking

- PHYLLIS DILLER says they made a movie about her cooking. "It's called *Grease*."
- She could dish it out—but she couldn't cook it.
- When she wants to punish her kids, she sends them to bed with dinner.

Cost of Living

- For most of us the cost of living will remain the same—about 15 percent more than we're making.

Counterfeiter

- A counterfeiter is a man who gets into trouble by following a good example.

Court

- A wife told the judge, "I always had his best interests at heart." The husband said, "Yeah? So how come she married me?"

Courtesy

- The only way to inspire courtesy on the road is to drive a police car.

C.P.A.

- An accountant is a guy who shows you how to save almost enough money to pay his bill.

Credit

- I still can't figure out how over a million people who are employed in the automobile industry can make a living from something nobody has paid for.

- VICTOR ATHOLZ: "In today's economy, one must give credit where cash is due."
- Today's woman knows you can't buy happiness—but you can charge it.
- I asked my neighbor if he lives within his income. He answered, "Certainly not. I have all I can do living within my credit."
- For the man who has everything: a calendar to remind him when the payments are due.
- Why steal when you can buy on credit and not pay like an honorable man?
- Times sure do change. In the old days men rode chargers—now they marry them.

Credit Cards

- The credit card bit has really gone crazy. The other night I saw a fella at a restaurant who wanted to pay cash. They wouldn't take it until he showed his American Express card and his driver's license.
- Credit cards are what people use when they discover that money can't buy everything.
- A credit card is a printed I.O.U.
- The advantage a credit card has over money is that it can be used over and over again.

Crime

- In New York, they no longer give anyone the key to the city. Instead, they have a guy come over who tells you how to pick a lock.
- There is one neighborhood in New York that is so tough you could walk ten blocks without leaving the scene of a crime.
- The old saying, "Crime doesn't pay," is a fake. *It pays.* There's only one way to stop it—let the government run it.

- Central Park had a very slow night last Saturday—so these two muggers mugged each other.
- Crime is when Congress meets.
- GOVERNOR CUOMO is against the death penalty. He's afraid the people will use it on politicians.
- Just remember that in this country a man is innocent until he's proven guilty—or fails to pay his attorney.
- There's plenty of crime in the streets. Especially in Washington, where it's not unusual to see three or more politicians together.
- The cop caught a robber who was sticking up stores in the daytime. The cop said, "How come you pull stickups in the daytime?" The robber said, "You think I'm crazy, walking around at night with all that money?"

Daffynitions
- Wisdom: Knowing what to do.
  Skill: Knowing how to do .
  Virtue: Not doing it.

Dating
- RAQUEL WELCH asked me out once. I was in her room at the time.

Daytime TV
- We owe a lot to daytime television. If it weren't for game shows and soap operas, millions of women would be out driving.

Death and Taxes
- Sometimes I wish they came in that order.

Debt
- The family that isn't in debt today is underprivileged.
- Running into debt doesn't bother me—it's running into creditors.

Democracy
- A democracy is a place where we have complete control over how we pay our taxes—cash, check, or money order.

Dentist
- All my dentist does is make appointments for me to see another dentist. I really don't know if he's a dentist or a booking agent.

Depression
- When your wife loses her job.

Détente
- Like going to a wife-swapping party and coming home alone.

Diamonds
- Are forever—and so are the payments.
- A diamond is the hardest substance known—to get back from a woman.

Dictionary
- Did you know that Webster wrote the dictionary because he had a nagging wife? Every time she opened her mouth he said, "What's that supposed to mean?"

Diet
- I found a diet that really works—it's called grocery bill.
- BESS MYERSON's diet program: "I keep putting off till tomorrow what I should be taking off today."
- Eat, drink, and be merry, for tomorrow they may be deductible. Or eat, drink, and be merry for tomorrow ye diet.
- With my wife, weighing is a religious experience. She steps on the scales and says, "Oh, my God!"
- You know you're getting fat when you get up from a metal chair and you have to fluff it up.
- It's easy to diet these days. Just eat what you can afford.
- A new diet candy is on the market. The ladies love it. Chocolate and nuts with a plain lettuce center.

- I have a friend who doesn't diet and never gains an ounce. He eats six meals a day. An average meal consists of two steaks, four pounds of potatoes, three hamburgers, an apple pie, a malted, an ice cream soda, and a hot fudge sundae . . . and he still weighs the same 475 pounds.
- There's a new tranquilizer diet. You don't lose weight, but you don't care about being fat anymore.
- More people would stop smoking if they'd prove cigarettes had calories.
- GENE BAYLOS says he's come up with a sure-fire reducing diet. He never eats while his wife is talking.
- PHYLLIS DILLER says, "Why should I lose weight? More people look like me than BO DEREK. Show me a dame with a beautiful body and I'll show you a hungry girl."
- My wife went to one of those diet doctors and in just three weeks she lost $6,000.
- BUDDY HACKETT told me his wife went on a new acupuncture diet. She doesn't eat anything; she loses weight through leakage.

Diplomacy

- The ability to take something and act as though you were giving it away.
- The art of letting someone else have your way.
- HENRY KISSINGER asks, "Do you want to know the difference between diplomacy and stupidity? It is this: If you tell a girl her face would stop a clock, that's stupid; but if you tell her 'When I look at your face, time stands still,' that's diplomacy."

Diplomat

- HENRY KISSINGER also says, Today a good diplomat is one who must speak a number of languages—including double-talk.
- A diplomat is an honest man sent abroad to lie for his country.
- A perfect diplomat praises married life but remains single.
- A diplomat's life centers around three things: protocol, alcohol, and Geritol.

Discos

- Disco dancing is an activity that requires a good rear for music.
- If you want to do the latest dance, just tie your shoelaces together and go.
- I think discos and those new dances are crazy. Kids don't look at each other, don't talk to each other, don't touch each other. It's like being married for thirty years.
- I don't like those wild dances. I like slow dancing when I'm dancing with a girl. I like to know what I'm up against.

Divorce

- Divorce isn't as easy as it used to be. I know one couple who got a divorce and the lawyers got the house.
- ZSA ZSA says, "Getting divorced just because you don't love a man is almost as silly as getting married just because you do."
- Woody Allen talks about love: "After six years of marriage, my wife and I couldn't decide whether to take a vacation or get a divorce. We decided that a trip to Bermuda is over in two weeks—but a divorce is something you always have."
- My neighbor ran away from his wife. There's a big argument about what he should be charged with. She claims it's desertion, he says it should be leaving the scene of an accident.
- Divorce is when a husband no longer has to bring the money home to his wife. He can mail it.
- She said, "Why should I give him a divorce? I'd only have to share my husband's money with his lawyer."
- One drunk said to the other, "We got a divorce because we were incompatible. My wife hated me when I was drunk, and I couldn't stand her when I was sober."
- Some people marry for love, some for money, but most for a short time.
- Divorce has done more to promote peace than the UN.
- Divorce is useless. You get married for lack of judgment, you get divorced for lack of patience, then you remarry for lack of money.
- You never hear about girls marrying a man for his money anymore—but they do divorce him for it.

- The chief cause of divorce is marriage.

Doctors

- I bought a used car from my doctor and I know it's in good shape. He told me he only used it to make house calls.
- The doctor said to his patient, "I'm happy to say that the crisis is over—that is, if you've got the $600."
- The patient told his doctor, "I don't smoke, drink, keep late hours, gamble, or fool around with girls." The doc said, "How can I cure you if you have nothing to give up?"
- The patient told the doctor he had shingles—so the doc tried to sell him aluminum siding.
- The nurse at the hospital said to the patient, "You're just what the doctor ordered—a patient with a good credit rating."
- "Did you recover from the operation?" "No, the doctor says I still have two more payments to make."
- It now costs more money to go to the hospital than it once cost to go to medical school.
- My neighbor told his doctor that he had ringing in his head. The doc gave him an unlisted head and told him if it rings, don't answer it.

Dogs

- RODNEY DANGERFIELD told me, "I was once trying to walk my dog as a way to meet girls, but it didn't work. The dog was too smart. It turns out he was using me to meet other dogs."

Doorman

- A doorman is a genius who opens your taxi door with one hand, helps you in with the other, and still has a hand left waiting for the tip.

Drinking

- DEAN MARTIN has come up with the perfect cure for a stiff neck: Rub it with alcohol—from the inside.
- DEAN also says, "I don't drink for personal, selfish reasons. I drink to make other people interesting."

- The curse of heavy drinking is when you get stuck with the tab.
- Why is it when you constantly drink to other people's health, you invariably ruin your own?

Drive-In

- You go to a drive-in theater and what do you see? Sex, perversion, sodomy—and then you look at the screen.
- There's a new drive-in theater screen. The manager puts one around each car.

Drunk Driving

- One way to cut down on drunk driving would be for the saloons to offer free home delivery.
- If you drink like a fish, swim—don't drive.

Dry

- There's a town in Australia called Cooktown. It's so dry, they have to pin the stamps on their letters.

Dumb-Dumbs

- Did you hear about the dumb-dumb mosquito that bit Dolly Parton on the arm?
- Everybody is ignorant—only in different subjects. Every country has its share of dumb-dumbs, but Slobbovia welcomes them all. Did you ever see a Slobbovian jigsaw puzzle? One piece.
- One Slobb took an I.Q. test and misspelled I.Q.
- What do you call a stork that delivers a Slobbovian baby? A dope peddler.
- Slobbovian men are very rough. I know one whose wife had twins. He went out with a shot gun looking for the other man.
- How about the Slobb who damaged his health by drinking milk? The cow fell on him.
- What happens when a Slobbovian housewife doesn't pay her garbage bill? They don't bring her any more . . .
- He was given a book for his birthday and he's still looking for the place to put in the batteries.

- He came home and found his wife in bed with his partner. "What are you doing?" he shouted. She said, "See? Didn't I tell you he was stupid!"

Earthquake

- They say the safest place to be during an earthquake is in a doorway. I figure if one ever hits New York, it's the hookers on Eighth Avenue who'll survive.

Economics

- A recession is when your neighbor loses his job. A depression is when you lost your job. A panic is when your wife loses her job.

Economist

- An economist is a man who knows more about money than people who have it.
- An economist is a man who tells you what to do with your money after you've done something else with it.

Economy

- If you think you've got troubles, the garment center is *really* in trouble. One manufacturer had to lay off three salesmen, four cutters, and his son-in-law.
- Two can live as cheaply as one large family used to.
- If GEORGE WASHINGTON never told a lie, what is he doing on a dollar bill that's worth 35 cents?
- I don't want to say our economy is bad, but it's now moving so slowly even the post office is getting jealous.
- The man who says he blew a fortune in the market just returned from a trip to his supermarket.
- Our son and daughter-in-law came up with a foolproof way to save money on food. They bought themselves an economy car and began driving over to our house for dinner.
- Everyone knows that a counterfeit dollar isn't worth the paper it's printed on. Unfortunately, it's getting to be true about a real dollar.

- If the economy doesn't improve soon, PRESIDENT REAGAN will be the first President to ride a horse into the unemployment office.
- A dollar these days will go further than you think. In fact, you can carry it around for days without finding anything you can buy with it.
- Money doesn't talk these days—it goes without saying.
- The wife was crying to her mother, "We always have too much month left at the end of our money."
- If you had to live your life over again you'd need more money!
- Look on the bright side of things. If the dollar loses it's value, think how sad it will make you feel when you send your ex-wife her alimony check.
- The role of the American male in our economy is to make almost as much money as his wife spends.

Efficiency Expert
- A man who is smart enough to tell you how to run your business but too smart to start one of his own.

Egghead
- A schmoe who has found something more interesting than a woman.

Egotist
- He's going to have a sex change operation so he can marry himself and have children.
- This actor is so conceited that on his last birthday he sent a letter of congratulations to his secretary.
- A man who thinks he is everything you think you are.
- The nicest thing about an egotist is that he never goes around talking about other people.

Elections
- They're held only to prove which poll was right.

Elizabeth Taylor
- Has three towels in her bathroom: His, Hers, and Who's Next?

Employment

- Things are tough in the job market. I met a guy who said he just lost his job. I said, "Where did you work?" He said, "The unemployment office."

Engagements

- ZSA ZSA said, "You know what I like about an engagement ring, darling? It's proof that love is not blind—at least, not stone-blind."

Escalators

- One employee told his boss he was late because he got stuck on the escalator in his building. "Why didn't you just walk down?" asked the boss. The employee said, "Because I was going up."

Executive

- He doesn't believe in wasting time with secretaries. He uses the old saying, "If at first you don't succeed—fire her!"

Exercise

- My wife's idea of exercise is to shop faster.

Experience

- An employer interviewing an applicant said, "You ask high wages for a man with no experience." The prospect replied, "It's so much harder work when you don't know anything about it."

Eyesight

- When it begins to blur, you should use stronger glasses and weaker drinks.

Family

- PAUL ARNSTEIN tells me, "My mother insisted my sister get married because she was in the family's way."

Farm

- A farm is a four-letter word meaning a piece of land that if you get up early enough and work hard enough it will make you a fortune—if you strike oil on it.

Farmers

- I heard milk prices are going up. So I went to farm country to see why the cows aren't contented.
- I want to tell you, those farmers live pretty good. "You must remember," one told me, "that the death rate in this community is the lowest in the state." I can believe that. I wouldn't want to be found dead there myself.
- Talk about young wives, those farmers marry out of kindergarten. One big spender gave his bride a rattle instead of an engagement ring. Their house didn't have a backyard—it had a playpen. I heard this farmer tell his wife of two years, "Another report card like this, Lucy, and I'm going to get a divorce from you."

Fashion

- Women's clothes are getting more masculine and men's clothes are getting more feminine. Pretty soon you'll be able to save a fortune by marrying someone your own size.
- Girls' jeans will come in three sizes this year: small, medium, and don't bend over.
- My neighbor's wife always wants to buy a new outfit every time they're invited out. He thought he'd play a big joke on her once and accepted an invite to a nudist wedding. The joke was on him. She spent $1,500 on a body lift.
- Fashion is a personal thing. PHYLLIS DILLER is the only girl I know who wears prescription underwear.
- SOPHIA LOREN says, "I don't like loose dresses—tents are for Boy Scouts."
- CINDY notes, "I saw some of those new bikini fashions. Why, I have earrings that cover more than that . . ."
- Note to women who wear slacks: Does your end justify your jeans?

- I saw one actress who wore so much padding that she didn't undress—she unpacked.

Faults

- Most people won't admit their faults. Me, I'd be glad to admit mine—if I had any.

Finances

- I know a fella who made a fortune in the market—$100,000, to be exact. He slipped on a grape in the supermarket and sued.

Financial Planning

- The man and wife were planning their will. The wife said lovingly, "When one of us dies, I'm going to Paris."

Florist

- Sign in a window of a Madison Avenue flower shop: "Sexy Flowers: Just Out of Their Beds."

Food

- These days all you can buy are frozen turkeys. The one we had in our freezer was so frozen stiff, for the first couple of hours in the oven he had a great time!"
- REVEREND AUSTIN MILES preaches, "They are selling horse-burgers in New York. That's really putting the a la carte before the horse."

Football

- The Arabs claim the football strike was started by a couple of Jewish boys who didn't want to touch pigskin.
- PUDGY hopes the professional football players win their strike but still feels some of them are making an outrageous demand—they want Sundays off.

Foreign Aid

- The President handed a big check to the head of a foreign country and said, "Here, fix your economy—and if it works, let me know what you did and we'll try it here."

Foreign Delegates

- One thing about those UN representatives—they are all sincere whether they mean it or not.

Foreign Languages

- Learning a foreign language is important because it enables you to talk back to your parents in two languages.

Foreign Policy

- On foreign policy, our dealings are an open book—a checkbook.
- Foreign affairs are great—if you don't give your real name.

Forger

- A person who is already ready to write a wrong.

Free

- The man who thinks the best things in life are free just hasn't been caught yet.

Free Love

- He asked her, "Do you believe in free love?" She said, "Have I ever given you a bill?"

Freedom

- Being able to do what you please without considering anyone except the wife, boss, police, life insurance company, state, federal, and city authorities, and the neighbors.

Friends

- He has no friends. He brought a parrot home and it told him to get out.

Frugality

- My neighbor is really frugal. He replaced the light bulb in the refrigerator with a candle.

Frustration

- Frustration is the first time you discover you can't do it the second time. Consternation is the second time you discover you can't do it the first time.

Gambling

- This guy went to see a psychiatrist to help him with his gambling problem, and it worked. "I used to go to the track every day—now I only go when it's open."
- Gambling is a way of getting nothing for something. The longest odds in the world are those against getting even.
- Most people are willing to gamble on anything. A lot of people I know are saving money on the premise that it may be valuable some day.
- My friend EARL WILSON was describing the '29 crash as, "A time when billions were lost and so many were ruined." MILTON BERLE interjected, "An average day in Las Vegas."
- ZSA ZSA has a tip for all wives to prevent their husbands from gambling: "Spend it first."
- Horse sense is what keeps horses from betting on what people will do.
- A real loser in Atlantic City is a guy who walks around the casino asking people if they want to buy a rented car.
- I hear it's estimated that Americans spend over $7 billion a year on games of chance alone. The interesting part of it is that this doesn't even include weddings, starting new businesses, or holding elections.

Garage

- The lady driver asked the mechanic, "Do you charge batteries here?" He said, "We sure do." She said, "Well, then put a new one in this car and charge it to my husband."

Garlic

- There's no such thing as a *little* garlic.

Gasoline

- The high cost of gasoline may wind up saving us money. By the time you fill the tank, you don't have money to go anywhere else.

Genius

- Someone who can do almost anything except make a living.
- A man who convinces his wife she looks vulgar in diamonds and fat in a fur coat.
- A stupid kid with proud grandparents.

Gigolo

- A fee-male.
- A guy whose ambition is to marry a rich girl who's too proud to let her husband work.
- A hired hand.

Girdles

- Woman who wear girdles don't have loose habits.
- PHYLLIS DILLER told me, "I got one of those new girdles that have magic fingers. Just my luck—mine had arthritis."

Golf

- The woman was complaining that her husband left her for the sixth time. Her friend consoled her: "Never mind, he'll be back again." She cried, "Not this time—he took his golf clubs with him."
- SAMMY KAYE bought a gasoline-driven cart and he asked the salesman, "Is it costly to run?" He said, "Not at all. You should be able to get at least three-hundred holes to the gallon."
- The man said, "My wife told me, either I sell my golf clubs or we get a divorce. I'm going to miss her."
- HOWARD GOLDEN insists New York is now the greatest city for golf nuts: "On the way to work every day, you can play eighteen potholes."

Good News

- Like the secretary said to the boss, "First the good news—you're not sterile."

Gossip

- Hear no evil, see no evil, speak no evil—and you'll never be a success at a cocktail party.
- Don't talk about yourself. It'll be done when you leave.
- A gossip is a person who will never tell a lie if the truth will do as much damage.
- MARY TYLER MOORE says, "Gossip is such a paradox. Some of the ugliest rumors start in beauty parlors."

Government

- I love my country—it's the government I can't stand.
- The government continues to spend more than it gets—because it's got confidence in us.

Government Spending

- My wife and the government have the same problem. They both like to do a lot of things they can't afford to do.

Governmental Machinery

- That's the marvelous labor-saving device that enables ten men to do the work of one.

Graduation

- The young man handed his diploma to his father and said, "Well, I've finished law school to please you and mom, now I'm going to be a fireman like I've been saying to you since I was six."

Gravity

- The teacher explained, "If you understand the law of gravity you'll understand what keeps us on Earth." One student asked, "How did we stick on before the law was passed?"

Gypsy Palm Reader

- A gypsy palm reader told a client, "You will be poor and unhappy until you are forty." "And then what?" asked the client. "Nothing," said the gypsy. "By that time you'll be used to it."

Happiness

- They say that BURT REYNOLDS has a yacht, a Rolls Royce, a jet plane, four horses, a few million dollars, and a different girl every week—*but is he happy*? You bet your life he is.
- Happiness is seeing your favorite girlfriend in a two-piece outfit—slippers.
- Happiness is when your girl sees you out with your wife and she forgives you.

Health

- RIP TAYLOR told me, "I'm in such bad shape that my health club makes me use the rear entrance."

Hecklers

- "Next time you give your old clothes away, stay with them."

Henpecked

- My uncle is so henpecked he's still taking orders from his first wife.

High Fashion

- No wonder they call it high fashion. Take a look at the price tags.

Higher Education

- Education is terrific. They teach a person to be literate so he can spell his name right on the unemployment forms.

Hindsight

- What a woman should have before wearing jeans.

History

- My neighbor says, "My kid refuses to study history any more. He claims they're making it faster than he can learn it."

Holidays

- Let's reflect on what this holiday has brought to all of us. More bills.

Hollywood

- One starlet took me up to her apartment to show me her etchings—and she sold me five etchings.
- The Beverly Hills Fire Department is so chic they spray Perrier water to put out the fires.
- CHARLTON HESTON says, "I'm happy with my life but everything is against me. I'm dull, square, Protestant, I'm not an alcoholic, and I've only had one wife. My kids are good human beings and I'm addicted to peanut butter. I'm just not good copy."

Hollywood Pal

- Someone who is always around when he needs you.

Hollywood Squares

- Until I saw "Hollywood Squares" on TV, I thought a Hollywood square was an actor who slept with his own wife.

Honeymoon

- The honeymoon is over when the husband gets out of the car at a drive-in movie to wipe off the windshield.
- The honeymoon is over when he stops helping her with the dishes—and starts doing them himself.

Horror Stories

- If you like a good horror story, go home and read your electric meter.

Horse Racing

- No horse can go as fast as the money you bet on him.

- My neighbor finally figured out a way to beat the first four races. He doesn't show up until the fifth.

Horseburgers

- One Manhattan vendor has this sign on his cart: "Try our delicious horseburgers—every one is a winner."

Hospitals

- No patient should leave a hospital until he's strong enough to face the cashier.
- "The nurses there are very possessive," my friend told me. "They always say, 'How's our leg today?' So I touched our knee and she slapped our face."
- A hospital room is a place where friends of the patient go to talk with other friends of the patient.
- I have a friend who just got out of the hospital. He tells me he got 500 get-well cards from Blue Cross alone.
- There should be an intensive care unit right next to the cashier's office.

Hotels

- Why are hotel room walls so thin when you sleep and so thick when you listen?
- The Grand Hyatt is a really big hotel. How big is it? Well, calling room service is long distance. And talking about room service—it was so slow, when I ordered breakfast, I had to leave a forwarding address.
- The new Harley Hotel is near the UN and it grabs the international set. In that lobby, English is a second language. There are so many foreigners in the hotel, you aren't allowed to drink the water.
- The new Milford Plaza attracts the traveling salesman, and, naturally my traveling salesman type jokes. Since the hotel is on Eighth Avenue, the new arrival was out on the street shopping the market looking for a particular piece of merchandise, preferably marked down. So he approached one little beauty on the corner and asked, "Do you speak English?"

She said, "A leetle beet." He asked, "A little bit, eh? How much?" She said, "Twenty-five dollar."

Housekeeper

- ZSA ZSA is the number-one housekeeper in America. Whenever she divorces a husband, she keeps the house.

Husbands

- CHER says, "Husbands are like fires. They go out when unattended."
- ROSEMARY CLOONEY notes, "A husband is a man who wishes he had as much fun when he's out as his wife thinks he does."
- JANE FONDA says, "A woman doesn't mind her husband being able to read a woman like a book, just as long as he does his studying between the right covers."

Hypochondriac

- You're a genuine hypo if, during TV commercials, you go to the medicine cabinet instead of the refrigerator.
- A hypochondriac is one who can't leave being well enough alone.

Ideal Husband

- The guy next door.

Ideal Man

- DORIS DAY says, "I can't understand why single girls go looking for the ideal man—when a husband is much easier to find."

Impossible

- A person who says nothing is impossible has never tried to remove bubble gum from an angora sweater.
- There are only two things that are really impossible: putting toothpaste back in the tube and getting off a mailing list.

Income

- All most men want from their wives? Affection, admiration, encouragement, and the ability to live grandly on an inadequate income.
- The trouble with marriage is, a fella can't support a wife and the government on one income.

Income Tax

- April 15 is a great religious holiday.
- You never see an atheist in the waiting room of the Internal Revenue Service.
- Income tax is the fairest tax of all. It gives everybody an equal chance at poverty.

Indians

- With all the murders, drug traffic, burglaries, and muggings, it seems to me the Indians should have had stricter immigration laws.
- The Indian checked into the nudist colony and set fire to the telephone booth. He wanted to send an obscene phone call.

Inflation

- Food, gas, rent, clothes, and Dolly Parton.
- Nowadays, when you order a $10 steak, you really get a mouthful.
- Apples are so costly that kids are now bringing a grape to the teacher.
- Did you notice that supermarkets don't deliver anymore? That's because Brink's doesn't have any refrigerated armored trucks.
- HILDEGARDE says, "Inflation is ruining us. I went to a store to buy a pair of pajamas. They wanted $200. I told them that for $200 the pajamas should come with a man in them."
- Only a few years ago, $50 used to feed a family of five. Today you're lucky if $50 can feed a child of five.
- I always pay my check at the restaurant as soon as I order, not

after dinner. That way I'm sure the prices won't go up during dinner.

- If you long for the good old days when you didn't have to worry about car payments—remember, you probably didn't have a car.
- You can be sure of one thing about this economy. If you had your life to live over, you surely would need more money.
- Remember those old-time dime novels? Well, they're still around—only now they sell for $10.95.
- JACKIE MASON points out that the value of the dollar is decreasing while the price of bread is going up. The moral is save bread.
- These days take-home pay can hardly survive the trip.
- Inflation is when nobody has enough money because everybody has too much.
- The recession shouldn't bother anybody who was a failure during the boom.
- My neighbor says, "It seems all my money goes for food. But the kids won't eat anything else."
- The other day I went into a fancy restaurant for lunch. By the time I got finished tipping the parking attendant, the hat check girl, the maitre d', and the waiter, my hot dog cost me $40.
- A quarter will buy you a nickel's worth of anything these days.
- It's easy making money these days. What's hard is making a living.
- My electric bill is so high I had to get a second mortgage on my fuse box.
- Remember when you paid $50 a plate for dinner and the money went to some charity instead of some restaurant owner?
- According to my life's savings I'm six years old. The fact that I'm past forty has nothing to do with it.
- Inflation, which used to be creeping, and then jogging, is now running wild.
- Prices are rising so fast that a dollar saved is 50 cents lost.
- I'm paying so much for wine, women, and song, I don't have money left over for luxuries.

- With today's prices, you shouldn't barbecue a steak—you should bronze it.
- Statistical analysis has shown that it costs more than $100 a mile to send an astronaut to the moon. This may seem expensive, but it compares very favorably with the cost of more than $500 a mile to push a shopping cart in a supermarket.
- MORTIMER COHEN suggests, "With food prices what they are today, I can make more money by not eating than by working."
- LOU JACOBI saw a sign in a window of a butcher shop: Sirloin Steak—Easy Payments.
- Gasoline is so expensive in New York that bank robbers have switched to getaway car pools.
- There are a lot of things money can't buy. For instance, what it bought last month.
- CARMINE SANTULLI says, "I tried to put my 2 cents into a discussion relating to our community and was told, 'The minimum is now $2.'"
- Sign in Bronx supermarket: "Big Sale! Everything Reduced to Last Week's Prices."
- Inflation is being broke with money in your pocket.
- If your income is below average and your spending is above, don't worry. You are average.
- Prices are ridiculous. You go to Cartier's and they have three things in the window: a diamond necklace, a sapphire brooch, and a lamb chop.
- We have the highest standard of living in the world. If only we could afford it.
- Sign in supermarket: Nobody Under $21 Admitted.
- The average man now lives ten years longer than he did in 1940. He has to, to get all his bills paid.

Inquisitive

- His wife told him she bought a new coat. "Another coat?" he screamed, "where will I get the money to pay for it?" She answered, "I may have a lot of faults, but I'm not inquisitive."

Insomnia

- I once had insomnia so bad I couldn't even sleep on the job.

Insult

- FRANK POPESIL talks about his neighbor: "The stork that brought him should be arrested for smuggling dope."

Insurance

- A manufacturer who was considering joining a lodge asked the president of one of them, "Does your lodge have any death benefits?" "It certainly does," the lodge president replied. "When you die, you don't have to pay any more dues."
- Honesty is the best policy—except when trying to collect on your insurance policy.
- My agent told me if I didn't buy a piece of his rock, he'd throw it through my windshield. So I bought a policy and now I really feel like I'm in good hands. I just wish they weren't around my neck.
- I've got a great insurance company: Mutual of Sicily.
- Life insurance is something that keeps a man poor all his life so he can die rich. Come to think of it, you got to be a nut to buy life insurance. Here's a guy betting you you're going to live and you're betting him you're going to die and you hope he wins and they charge you for thinking like that.
- The insurance salesman said to me, "Don't let me frighten you into a hasty decision. Sleep on it tonight. If you wake up tomorrow, let me know."
- What really hurt Humpty-Dumpty wasn't that he had a great fall, but that he had recently let his accident insurance lapse.

Interest Rates

- They're getting ridiculous. I know one clothing store that charges 10 percent interest when you pay cash.

Invasion

- The Russians will never invade the United States—they couldn't afford to live here.

Iran

- Did you know that in Iran you could talk your head off?

Iranian Justice

- It's the death penalty for adulterers and sex offenders; the amputation of fingers and hands for related crimes. Imagine what they would cut off if BURT REYNOLDS lived there?

IRS

- The American public owes a lot to the I.R.S.—ulcers, nausea, and diarrhea.
- Every man's income runs into four figures. The real one, the one he reports to the IRS, the one he tells his wife, and the one he tells the boys at the club.

Israel

- You've got to give Israel credit. The only thing chicken about them is their soup.

Italian Coffee

- FRANK SINATRA says, "The only trouble with Italian coffee is that a week later you're asleep again."

Jogging

- These days it's hard to tell whether a runner is someone who is jogging to reduce or a motorist who is reduced to jogging.
- My doctor told me jogging would add years to my life. He was right. I feel ten years older already.
- "Jogging is good for you," the doctor told me. I get tired sealing an envelope. The odds on me getting in shape are about the same as a photographer catching NANCY REAGAN in a housedress.

Jealous

- I've often wondered why a man who hasn't made love to his wife in five years will kill a man who does it for him.

Joint Accounts

- The lady cried, "My husband accuses me of overdrawing our checking account. I haven't overdrawn. He has under-deposited."

Jokes

- There are only a few original jokes, and most of them are in Washington.

Justice

- A man was sued for divorce on the grounds that he was sterile. About the same time, he was sued by their maid for being the father of her child. He lost both cases.

Kids

- What's the use of teaching your kid to talk when in a few years you'll wish he'd shut up.
- A little girl ran into the classroom and told the teacher, "Two boys are fighting out on the playground, teacher, and I think the one on the bottom would like to see you."
- DR. BENJAMIN SPOCK advises, "Watch the kid who's cutting classes at school. He may be in training to be a congressman."
- For most kids an unbreakable toy is something you use to smash those that aren't.
- My nephew is nine years old. He told his mother, "I fell on my keister today." Mom said, "You should not use language like that." The boy said, "But RONALD REAGAN uses it." She said, "So don't play with him."
- The hardest part about telling young people about the facts of life is finding something they don't already know.
- Kids have it made. Their mothers drive them everywhere. They

drive them to school, to their friends' houses, to the movies, to the bowling alley, and to dancing lessons. I know one kid who wanted to run away from home and his mother said, "Wait, I'll drive you."

- BOB NEWHART notes: "Kids used to ask you where they came from—today they tell you where to go."

Kosher

- JACKIE MASON teaches, "Did you know in my religion the sin of eating bread on Passover is comparable to the sin of adultery? I told this to a friend and he says he tried them both and can't see the comparison."

Labor

- RIP TAYLOR told me, "I had to quit my job at a bloomer factory. I was only pulling down one hundred fifty a week.
- I was a labor organizer in a maternity ward.
- The Secretary of Labor says there is no unemployment problem. It's just a rumor started by thousands of people who are out of work.
- The unions are fighting for a four-day week. What's the fight? Most workers are already working a four-day week—only it takes them five days to do it.
- There are no strikes in Russia. Come to think of it, we've got more people on strike than they have working.
- Max the plumber was summoned to a mansion to fix a leak, and tried to combine business with pleasure with the pretty maid. She refused on the grounds that her mistress was home and she didn't want to get fired. Next morning, she called him to say her mistress was out, and would he like to come over and see her. "What!" yelled Max. "On my own time?"
- Nobody wants to make house calls anymore. I called an exterminator to ask if he could kill roaches and he said, "Sure. When can you bring them over?"
- Arriving several hours late, the plumber inquired, "How have

you managed?" The woman replied, "Not badly. While we were waiting for you to get here, I taught the children to swim!"

- The plumber said, "I've come to fix your pipes." The lady said, "I didn't call a plumber." He growled, "Aren't you Mrs. Schwartz?" She said, "No. She moved away a year ago!" He said, "How do you like that? They ask for a plumber, claiming its an emergency, and then they move!"

The Last Word

- The only time a man has the last word with a woman is when he apologizes.

Lawyers

- He's a great lawyer. I got a traffic ticket and he had it reduced to second-degree manslaughter.
- Some men inherit money, some earn it, and some are lawyers.
- The woman said, "I want something to calm my nerves." He said, "But I'm a lawyer, not a doctor." She said, "I know. I want a divorce."
- The lawyer was walking down Fifth Avenue when he saw the two cars collide. He rushed over and yelled, "I'm a lawyer. I saw the whole thing—and I'll take either side."
- If you can't get a lawyer who knows the law, get one who knows the judge.
- When a student first enters law school, he is provided with a huge book containing the subjects to study. The table of contents reads like this: Pages 1-20 Libel Laws . . . Pages 21-25 Divorce Laws . . . Pages 26-40 Criminal Laws . . . Pages 41-566 Loopholes.

Lecture

- Jones was brought to night court for being drunk and causing a disturbance. The judge asked, "Where were you going at 4 o'clock in the morning?" The drunk said, "To a lecture." The judge asked, "At 4 in the morning?" Jones said, "Sure, sometimes my wife stays up even later than that."

Lending Money
- Don't lend money to friends—it causes amnesia.

Liars
- So, big deal, GEORGE WASHINGTON never told a lie. But, for those of us who don't have cherry trees, it's become a way of life.
- You can always tell if a politician is telling the truth or not. If his lips are moving, he's lying.
- A sincere politician will never tell a lie—if the truth will cause more damage.
- Washington was first in war and first in peace, but if he never lied, honest George would never make it in politics today.
- It's January and it'll be interesting to see what the politicians break first—their New Year's resolutions or their campaign promises.
- RONALD REAGAN's not a typical politician because he doesn't know how to lie, cheat, or steal. He's always had an agent for that.
- My friend told me, "I'm really a loser. What a day I had. I lost my job. I lost my wallet. My wife ran away with my neighbor. The Mets lost to the Dodgers. It's unbelievable. Leading by three in the eighth, and they lost to the Dodgers."
- The income tax has made more liars of the American people than golf has.
- I asked one famous author, "Which of your works of fiction do you consider best?" He said, "My last income tax return."
- The witness was telling the judge, "I swore to tell the truth, but every time I do, some lawyer objects."
- I got a great lawyer. It's just that I don't even believe him when he swears he's lying.
- With a man a lie is a last resort—with a woman it's first aid. The judge said to the defendant, "You are lying so clumsily that I would advise you to get a lawyer."

- Some women find it hard to tell a lie—others can tell it as soon as their husbands open their mouths.
- The world's most common lie used to be, "Your check is in the mail." Now, it's, "Our computer is down."

Liberals

- Liberals are opposed to higher defense spending. Their idea of disarmament is taking guns away from the military and giving them to muggers.
- A liberal is a person who makes enemies left and right.

Life Insurance

- Fun is the same as life insurance. The older you get, the more it costs.

Life of the Party

- My neighbor says, "My wife and I are always the life of the party, but it isn't always the same party."

Limericks

- There was a young lady named Clair
Who possessed a magnificent pair,
Or that's what I thought,
Till I saw one get caught
On a thorn and begin losing air.
- There once was a fellow called Babbitt
Who made love to the girl as a habit;
But he ran for the door
When the girl asked for more
And explained, "I'm a man not a rabbit."
- Jack be nimble, Jack be quick,
Jack jumped over the candlestick.
Alas, he didn't clear the flame,
And now he's known as Auntie Mame.
- There was a great redhead from Lithem
Who sang with a band and slept with 'em.
It's sad to relate
She's borne twelve kids to date,

Six brass, four reeds, and two rhythm.

- There was a smart waitress in Reno
  Who lost all her dough playing Keno
  But she had the great knack
  To lay on her back
  And now she owns the casino.

Losers

- A guy who would marry RAQUEL WELCH for her money.
- A jack of all trades—and out of work in every one of them.
- An accordion player in a topless girl band.
- Rabbits' feet are lucky for everybody except rabbits.
- A loser is a guy who wrecks his automobile while driving home from the bank after making his final car payment.
- My secretary told me, "I guess I'm the kind of girl who just can't do anything right. Last week I kissed a prince and he changed into a frog."
- RODNEY DANGERFIELD made a fortune being a loser: "I had a terrible childhood," Rodney explains, "My parents didn't want me around. Other parents punished their kids for sneaking out of the house. Mine punished me for staying home." Rodney says, "The first time at the beach my old man gave the lifeguard $5 to keep an eye *off* me."
- STEVE MITTLEMAN admits he's a loser: "I'm the kind of guy whose twin sister forgot my birthday. . . . I got married and wasn't in any of the wedding pictures. . . . I set the house on fire when I was a kid and I was sent to my room."
- The lady was a loser. She took a cruise to meet some men and they seated her at a table with women only. She complained to the captain and asked to be put with some nice bachelors. The captain said, "Of course, madam." That evening, looking her prettiest, she swept into dinner and found the captain was true to his word. At her new table she was greeted by seven smiling priests!

Love

- "Dear Frankie," the loving letter began, "I haven't been able to sleep ever since I broke our engagement. Won't you forget and forgive? Your absence leaves a void nobody else could ever fill. I love you. I need you. I want you. Your loving Marian. P.S. Congratulations on winning the million dollar lottery."

- A girl in the hand is worth two on the phone.
- He loved her dearly and set out to prove it. He swam the deepest river. He crossed the widest desert. He climbed the highest mountain. She divorced him—he was never home.
- Bernie says his wife loves to talk while she's making love. "She calls me from the motel."
- JOHN TRAVOLTA says, "Love is like eating a mushroom. By the time you know whether it's the real thing, it's too late."
- Love, like the measles, attacks only the young.
- It is better to have loved and lost—provided no alimony is involved.
- A girl can learn to love a man—depending on how much he's willing to spend on her education.

Love and Marriage

- JOHN TRAVOLTA says, "I'm an unashamed old-fashioned romantic. I believe in love and marriage, but not necessarily with the same person."
- An old Arabic proverb: "Love is not a disease, and marriage is not a cure."

Love at First Sight

- "Where did you find that gorgeous girl?" I asked my old friend. He said, "I opened my wallet and there she was."

Love Thy Neighbor

- Love thy neighbor—but do not make love to her.
- Love thy neighbor—but first draw the blinds.

Lover

- They say a good lover can ignite sparks by the way he kisses. But just because a guy can light a stove—it doesn't necessarily make him a good cook.

Lover's Leap

- The distance between twin beds.

Luck

- He said his wife left him on Friday the 13th and she took everything. His friend said, "You're lucky—my wife didn't leave."

Madam

- One who offers vice to the lovelorn.

Marriage

- ROD STEIGER says, "To me marriage is an adventure. It's like going to war."
- DONNY OSMOND says, "My wife and I have a deal. If I don't like the way she does something, I can do it myself."
- For every man who marries for money, there's a gal who marries for alimony.
- It takes two to make a marriage—a single girl and an anxious mother.
- MICHAEL LANDON notes, "Life is full of coincidences. Have you noticed that it takes two to make an argument and the same number to get married?"
- MILTON OLAN says, "My wife would make a very good soccer goalie. I haven't scored in months."
- "My wife says I'm bisexual. I do it twice a month."
- Let's face it, even in this swinging modern age, a man still needs a wife. He has socks to mend, clothes to wash, and buttons to be sewn on. And a wife knows where to have those things done.
- All marriages are happy. It's the living together afterward that's tough.
- Guest's comment at a wedding: "They'll make a perfect couple. She's a hypochondriac and he's a pill."
- RICHARD CHAMBERLAIN explains, "People often ask why I never married. My answer is simple. I'm all for the battle of the sexes. I just don't believe in taking prisoners."

- The mother said to her daughter that was leaving, "Remember, marriage is give and take. If he doesn't give what you want—take it!"
- A successful man is one who earns more than his wife can spend; a successful woman is one who finds such a man.
- "Of course my wife and I are compatible," the husband told his analyst. "In fact, we both like the same thing. It's just that I like to save it and she likes to spend it."
- The bachelor who is beginning to get thin on top should marry the woman who is beginning to get fat on the bottom.
- One couple I know has a plan that seems to work. One night a week he goes out with the boys. The other six nights she does.
- My wife says that she only asked for pin money. But the first pin she wanted had twelve stones in it.
- She raved, "I can't stand it anymore, I want a divorce." The husband said, "You think I treated you like a dog!" She screamed, "No! A dog has a fur coat."
- "It doesn't bother me if my wife dreams of being married to a billionaire—as long as she doesn't do it while she is out shopping."
- My neighbor says, "Me and my wife have a perfect understanding. I don't try to run her life and I don't try to run mine."
- Many guys are experimenting with a lifestyle that involves living together without sex. It's called marriage.
- When you marry someone to share your troubles—you have twice as many troubles as when you were single.
- A lot of marriages these days are held together by the children. Both parents are afraid they'll wind up with them.
- Marriage is an arrangement by which two people agree to be polite to each other in public.
- Marriage is a great instructor. It teaches you loyalty, tolerance, understanding, perseverance, and a lot of other things you wouldn't need if you had stayed single.
- CLINT EASTWOOD says, "They say marriages are made in heaven —but so are thunder and lightning."
- BILLY GRAHAM says, "There are still more marriages today than divorces, which proves that preachers can still outtalk lawyers."

- MRS. BILLY GRAHAM notes, "Marriage is an institution held together by three books: The Good Book, the cookbook, and the checkbook."
- HENRY WINKLER said it: "A marriage license is the only license taken out after the hunt is over."
- The latest statistics indicate that more and more couples are living together before getting married; such a relationship is called a "trial marriage." I know I'll sound old-fashioned, but I just don't believe in trial marriages. I think they're very dangerous. If you're not careful, they can lead to the real thing!
- Every man needs a wife—because too many things go wrong you can't blame on the government.
- MARY MARTIN said it: "Marriage is a mutual admiration society in which one person is always right and the other is always the husband."
- ERIK ESTRADA: "The problem with girls who can be had for a song is that it often turns out to be 'The Wedding March.'"
- "Marriage is like a lottery," says FRANK SINATRA. "The trouble is, you can't tear up your ticket if you lose."
- LIBERACE says, "People sometimes ask me why I never got married, and I tell them the answer is simple. I'd rather go through life wanting something I didn't have, than having something I didn't want."
- Marriage is a wonderful institution. If it weren't for marriage, husbands and wives would have to fight with perfect strangers.
- My neighbor's wife was complaining about her missing husband: "I'm so miserable without him, it's like he's still here."

Marriage Counselor

- After they had been discussing their problems for a couple of hours, the prissy English lady said to the marriage counselor, "I think it's unfair to suggest that I don't enjoy sex. But what can you say about a man who wants it five or six times a year?"
- My neighbor told me, "My wife and I got some bad news—our marriage counselor is getting a divorce."
- "Don't you two have anything in common?" the marriage

counselor asked. "Yes," said the wife, "I can't stand him, and he can't stand me!"

Meat Packer

- Girdle manufacturer.

Medicare

- The way Medicare is going, in 1984 it will pay for dentists, in 1985 it will pay for psychiatrists, and in 1986 it will pay for get-well cards.

Medicine

- RIP TAYLOR says, "I'm not feeling too well—I just got a kidney transplant from a bed wetter."
- If only doctors were as good at relieving your cold symptoms as they are at relieving you of money.

Memory

- RODNEY DANGERFIELD says, "My wife says I have a bad memory. So far this year, I forgot her birthday, our anniversary—and who's boss."

Men and Women

- "To a smart girl, men are no problem—they're the answer," says BARBARA WALTERS.

Miami

- A tourist recently told me he likes Miami because of its diversity and uniqueness. It's the only place in the world where you can shake a tree and six oranges—and twelve Cubans—fall out.

Middle Age

- That's the period when a man's hairline goes back and his waistline goes forward.
- Middle age is when you have more fun remembering what you did than what you're doing.

- When a man is warned to slow down by his doctor instead of by a policeman.
- You have reached middle age when weight lifting consists of just standing up.
- The really frightening thing about middle age is the knowledge that you'll outgrow it.
- A man's feelings for women begin to turn to thoughts when he reaches fifty.
- Middle age is that time in life when women don't mind a guy who kisses and tells. They figure that at that age they need all the advertising they can get.
- You know you've reached the age of no return when you realize your father was right when he said it's as easy to fall in love with a rich girl as a poor one.

Mini-Skirt
- A tempt-dress.

Minority Rule
- A perfect example is a baby in the house.

Misers
- I used to think the word for anyone who hoarded money was a "miser." These days, anyone who hoards money is a "magician."

Mistress
- Like a wife, only she doesn't do the dishes.
- The difference between a mistress and a wife is the difference between night and day.

Modern Art
- What you buy to cover a hole in the wall—and then you find out the hole looked better.

Money

- There are more important things than money—but women won't date you if you don't have any.
- You never know the real value of money until you try to borrow some.
- Money isn't everything—but it's mighty handy if you don't have a credit card.
- The guy who said money isn't everything was almost right—it's nothing.
- The trouble with finances today is that when you're rich it's usually on paper and when you're broke it's in cash.
- They say money isn't everything. It won't buy health, it won't buy happiness, and it won't buy love. I say, give me the money and I'll rent them!

Motel

- I stopped at a motel that should have had a sign outside, "Washington couldn't sleep here."

Mothers

- One husband suggested, "One of the most valuable gifts to send your mother-in-law on Mother's Day is her daughter."
- A pal of mine left his wife because of another woman—her mother.
- The new bride gushed to her mother, "Joe is so good to me. He gives me everything I ask for." Mom said, "That merely shows you're not asking enough."
- A mother is someone who first says, "no," then thinks of a good reason.
- Sunday is Mother's Day. I hope you all remember to bring your mother presents and love. After all, what is home without a mother? A mess!
- My neighbor's wife just had her twelfth child and she's running out of names—to call her husband.
- And now a special word to all you children that have been pesty, do something that will really help your mother have a happy day—*leave*.
- Mother's Day is a little confusing in Hollywood. Most kids

play it safe out there. They send a card to their current mother, their previous mother, their original mother—and just to make sure, they also deliver one to the leading lady of their father's new picture.

Mother-in-Law

- MUHAMMED ALI says, "A mother-in-law is like a boxing referee—she often turns out to have an interest in one of the fighters."

Movies

- There's one thing you have to admit about today's movie theaters—there's usually more trash on the screen than on the floor.
- Movies today are terrifying. I went to one the other day, and I never saw such violence, sex, and vulgar language—and that was just at the popcorn stand.
- The sign at the movie window said, "Five dollars. Popular prices." The moviegoer asked the cashier, "You call $5 a popular price?" She said, sweetly, "WE like it."

Music Lover

- Some women are music lovers—others can love without it.

Neatness

- She's so tidy, when her husband makes love to her she complains he's messing up the bed.

New Year's Eve

- There's only one trouble with kissing the one you love best—some of those mirrors are cold!

New York City

- Mayor Koch's pooper-scooper law is working. Yesterday I saw a St. Bernard with a roll of Charmin around his neck.
- The mayor is on a keep New York beautiful kick: "Plant flowers in a pothole." He is putting up signs all over Manhat-

tan: "Keep New York clean—take your trash to New Jersey."

- I admit we are all suffering from the hardening of the traffic arteries. JERRY LEWIS says, "The last time I went to New York it was incredible. We circled the airport for hours. What made it incredible was, we were in a bus."
- JAN MURRAY says that the traffic in New York is so bad, rescue planes had to drop supplies to the Good Humor man.
- MILTON BERLE says, "The best way to kill an hour in New York City is to drive around the block."
- Forget the drive-in theaters—what we need are drive-in streets.
- New York City is such a friendly city. People are always dropping in—sometimes even when you're home.
- From the song, "We trip the light fantastic on the sidewalks of New York," a New Yorker says, "It's easy to trip these days with all the potholes and cracks in the sidewalks of New York."
- FREDDIE ROMAN says, "They purchased New York over 300 years ago for $24. It's now worth less."
- This town is the greatest. Where else can you see somebody invest in the stock market with a welfare check?

Nonchalance

- The ability to keep talking in an interesting manner while your friend is paying the check.

Nudist

- The nudist bride didn't go in the sun for three months—she wanted to be married in white.
- An engaged couple in the nudist colony decided to break up after six months. He explained, "We've been seeing too much of each other."
- I wonder what a nudist does with his keys after he locks his car.

Nudity

- The way the shows are going, and the movies, and cable TV, how are they going to top all the nudity next season? The actors are going to be covered and the audience will be nude.
- The big thing in movies today is male nudity.

- Seems the only thing they're zipping today is addresses.

Obscene
- I just got an obscene telephone call from the phone company. They want me to pay my bill.

Old Age
- Have you noticed that you have to get old before anybody will say you look young?
- Growing old has its compensations. All the things you couldn't have when you were young you no longer want.
- I've given up going to discos. My doctor says if I shake my booty one more time I'm gonna break it—and at my age it's pretty hard to find new parts.
- He's really getting old. He played the slot machine and it came out three prunes.
- By the time you learn to read girls like a book, your library card has expired.
- GEORGE BURNS: "A minister recently asked me why I thought God has permitted me to reach the ripe old age I have. I told him it's probably just to test the patience of my relatives." George adds, "Old age is when a man wakes up tired and lustless."
- That's the time of life when a woman buys herself a see-through nightgown and then finds she doesn't know anybody who can still see through one.

Old Maid
- A woman who has been good for nothing.

Old-Timer
- One who remembers when sex was not a spectator sport.
- A guy who remembers when 5 & 10 stood for cents instead of dollars.

Optimist and Pessimist
- If it weren't for the optimist, the pessimist wouldn't know how happy he isn't.

- A pessimist nowadays is a man who really knows what's going on. An optimist is a man who hasn't yet read the morning papers.
- An optimist is anybody who doesn't give a damn what happens—as long as it happens to somebody else.
- An optimist is always able to laugh at *your* troubles.
- "Love is responsible for most of the optimists, and marriage for most of the pessimists."
- The poor soul was screaming at his cheerful friend, "Happy? What have I to be happy about. I can't even pay my bills." The optimist said, "In that case, be thankful that you're not one of your creditors."
- My neighbor says, "If you have to have your eyes examined to get a driver's license, you should have your head examined before you get a marriage license."
- With the state of the world right now, if pessimists ain't happy today, they ain't never going to be.
- A pessimist is a man who feels all women are bad—an optimist hopes so.

Orgy
- Group therapy.

Oscars
- This is the time of the year when some Hollywood actors get ulcers wondering if they're going to get Oscars.

Parking
- It now costs $16 a day to put your car in a midtown garage in Manhattan. Or as Shakespeare might put it: "Parking is such sweet sorrow."
- When a tugboat towed the *Queen Elizabeth II* out of her Hudson River slip, a drunk sighed, "Boy, nowadays nobody can park anywhere."

Party

- I invited CHRISTINE JORGENSON and RENEE RICHARDS to my "come-as-you-were" party.
- Help preserve wild life—throw a party tonight.

Pay TV

- Pay TV is here to stay—I just got the bill from the repairman.
- What really got me mad was when my TV repairman sent me a card from a resort hotel *I* couldn't afford.

Peace

- HELEN REDDY said it: "The problem with today's peace movement is they seem to forget that the world will never be peaceful as long as half its inhabitants are men and the other half are women."

Perfect Figure

- In the Wall Street brokerage offices the perfect figure is 36¼-24⅛-35¼.

Philanthropist

- A guy who gives away what he should be giving back.
- One who gives away publicly what he stole personally.

Platonic Love

- Like eating soup with a fork.

Playboy

- He's real broad-minded. Even as an infant he grabbed for the nurse instead of the bottle.

Playgirl

- She does it for friends only—and she doesn't have an enemy in the world.

Police Department

- CARMINE SANTULLI agrees with me that we have the greatest

police department in the world—but "history repeats itself in the N.Y.P.D. Could it be 'small graft warnings ignored'?"

Polite

- My uncle is in jail for being too polite. He opened a car door for his wife. Of course, they were going 60 mph at the time.

Politics

- My neighbor says he hates busing: "My daughter was forced to go to school with a minority group—*Democrats.*"
- In a recent poll, 42 percent of the voters approved of the job REAGAN is doing, 30 percent were not happy, and 28 percent tried to borrow money from the guy taking the poll.
- Politics is not a bad profession. If you succeed there are many rewards. If you disgrace yourself or go to jail, you can always write a book.
- Politicians are divided into three groups: the anointed, the appointed, and the disappointed.
- In crime, the theory is take the money and run. In politics, it's run—and then take the money.
- The only people not allowed to hold elected office are lunatics and convicted felons. I always thought it was the other way around.
- One girl said to another, "What I'm looking for is a man who will treat me as if I were a voter and he was a candidate."
- It's useless to try and hold a person to anything he says while he's in love, drunk, or running for office.
- Politics is a game of give and take, with more takers than givers.
- Politics is the art of obtaining money from the rich and votes from the poor, on the pretext of protecting each from the other.
- There's a bill now that will solve this latest problem, if passed. It will make all bribes to public officials taxable.
- What would happen if everybody believed what political candidates say about each other and nobody won?
- RONALD REAGAN said it: "Personally, I think I like being in

Washington, D.C., better than in Hollywood, because here I get to write the script too!"

- Every politician is out to make a name for himself. Most of these names can't be printed in a family newspaper.
- There are two sides to every question—and a good politician takes both.
- A politician is the fellow who is always ready to lay down *your* life for *his* country.
- You rarely see a thin politician. It's because of all those words they have to eat.
- Most politicians suffer from the same problem—too much bone in the head and not enough in the back.
- A good politician knows how to say nothing. He just doesn't always know when. He can talk for an hour without mentioning what he was talking about.
- The trouble with most of today's politicians is that they try to show us they're part of the common herd by throwing us a lot of bull.
- The secret of politicians is, never open your mouth unless you have nothing to say.
- Give a politician enough rope—and he'll hang you.

Pollution

- If the pollution continues, walking on water will no longer be a miracle. Anybody will be able to do it.
- The air in California is so bad—especially in Hollywood—that even the coke sniffers are using filter-tipped straws.

Poor

- CARMINE SANTULLI says, "I know what it is to be poor. I was once a poor boy—now I'm a poor man."

Population Explosion

- The population explosion would probably be much less of a problem if setting the fuse wasn't so much fun.

Pornography

- A member of the vice squad arrested a peddler on 42nd Street for selling pornographic photographs. "But these aren't dirty," the salesman complained. The officer pointed to one particularly intricate study of several naked men and women. The guy said, "Ain't you ever seen five people in love before?"
- Pornography is a major problem in our society, especially when you can't afford it.
- The board of education explains how to keep pornography out of the hands of teenagers: "Put it in textbooks. They'll never find it there."

Post Office

- Congress is considering selling advertising on our postage stamps to cover the deficit. Somehow, I don't know if I'm quite ready for a 20-cent stamp featuring the Statue of Liberty dressed in a pair of Calvin Klein jeans.
- It costs us 20 cents to mail a letter, but nobody says how much it costs to get it delivered.
- I wrote a letter to the postmaster telling him how to improve the service at the post office. But the letter got lost.
- I can't understand it. If people travel faster by air, how come the mail moves slower?
- The postal service wants to increase the price of a first class stamp from 20 cents to 25 cents. But they've got a good reason. You see, they've been receiving so many letters of complaint about their having raised the rates from 18 cents to 20 cents that they have to raise them again to make it so people can't afford to keep mailing them letters of complaint.
- At the rate they're going, stamps go up before the letter gets there. I get junk mail with postage due. First-class postage was increased about 75 percent in the last few years. Now when you begin a letter with "Dear," you mean it. I could make a fortune if I opened a post office.
- The post office has a new motto: "Neither rain nor sleet, nor dark of night shall stay these couriers from the swift comple-

tion of their appointed rounds. But if it's this hot again tomorrow—forget it."

- People usually get what's coming to them—unless, of course, it's mailed.
- I don't want to say the mail is slow—but last week my flower seeds arrived as a bouquet.
- The postal service is so slow. My grandfather wrote to the White House to complain, and he just got back a very nice reply—signed by Calvin Coolidge.
- If the world is getting smaller, why do they keep raising the postal rates?
- The post office is promoting "express mail." That means they'll guarantee to lose your letter the same day you mail it.

Poverty

- Join the campaign to end poverty. Send money.
- I saw this sign on the front door of an apartment house in the Bronx: "This property is protected by poverty—nothing in the building is worth stealing."

Practical Nurse

- The one who marries a rich patient.

Premarital Relations

- The only premarital activities women don't participate in these days is cooking.

Problem Drinkers

- Those who never buy.

Profits

- Income that the IRS has temporarily overlooked.

Propaganda

- Baloney disguised as food for thought.

Prostitution

- New York is having a big problem with ladies of the evening. And if you're wondering why they're called ladies of the evening—have you ever seen one in the daylight?
- "Would you please lend me $50 until I get back on my back?"
- A prostitute may be good for nothing—but she's never bad for nothing.

Protein

- A call girl too young to vote.

Prude

- She's such a prude that she blushes when somebody says "intersection."

Psychiatrist

- The handsome prisoner said to the gorgeous prison shrink, "I have this mad urge to grab you and crush you in my arms." She said, "*Now* you're talking sense."
- Psychiatry is very helpful, especially to the psychiatrists.
- Doctor Gelt has this sign up in his office: "Your financial obligation does not end with suicide."
- My friend Howard was put under the care of a noted Park Avenue shrink. "How soon will I be cured?" he asked. The doc said, "As soon as you run out of money."
- Seeing a psychiatrist cured his drinking problem. The sessions cost so much, he couldn't afford to buy liquor anymore.
- You can't win. My shrink told me to speak freely. After my monologue was over, he charged me $50.
- "Do you know how many psychiatrists it takes to change a light bulb?" . . . "No. How many?" . . . "Just one. But it takes a very, very long time because the light bulb has to really want to change."
- This fella went to a psychiatrist and complained, "Doc, you gotta help me. I'm involved in a shipboard romance." The doc said, "What's so unusual about a shipboard romance?" He said, "I'm in the navy."

- The eighty-year-old lady told the doctor, "I have a problem. My husband is losing his potency and I'd like to know if the condition is psychogenic or physical?" The doc asked, "How old is your husband?" She said "Eighty-three." He asked, "Well, when did you first notice he was losing his potency?" She said, "I first noticed it last night—and again this morning."

Psychoanalysis

- Is spending $50 an hour to squeal on your mother.

Psychology

- The science that tells you what you already know, in words you can't understand.

Public Service

- There's a new game in Washington called Public Service. Everybody stands around and the first one to do something loses.

Puns

- A pun is the lowest form of humor. It's outrageous, sick, childish, stupid, ridiculous—that is, if you didn't think of it first.
- The first pun is credited to ADAM. EVE teased him, "What's wrong with eating this little ole apple?" And Adam answered, "I'll bite." That's what got them both bounced out of the Garden of Eden.
- And how about CLEOPATRA, who cried, "I want my mummy."
- Harry thought he recognized a girl at the bar. "Is that Hortense?" he asked. "She looks relaxed to me."
- This girl had a breast enlargement operation and was delighted with the results. She wrote a letter to her doctor, "Thanks for the mammaries."
- SAMMY KAYE tells me one musician worked for him and borrowed so much money, all he would play were promissory notes.

- BOB HOPE says, "Bilious is a feeling you get when you open your mail on the first of the month." I really expected better from Bob.

Putdowns
- MILTON BERLE said to me, "I may not agree with you—but I'll defend your right to shut up."
- Two ladies met at a dinner party. "You don't remember me?" . . . "Oh yes," she answered sweetly, "We met two years ago. I never forget a dress."

Reading
- The man who can read women like a book usually likes to read in bed.

Readjustment
- When your colleague loses his job.

President Reagan
- Says we need a man who can talk back to the Russians. I met a thousand taxi drivers who'll do that.
- I hope Reagan stops being an actor and starts to produce.
- President Reagan is carrying his cowboy image too far. When he signs legislation he uses a branding iron.
- Nothing can stop Reagan from running again. What ham actor can resist a sequel?
- Proved a *B* actor can become an *A* President. "In an economy move," says BERNIE COOPER, "he fired his White House servants and replaced them with Bonzo and relatives. They work for bananas."

Reganomics
- PRESIDENT REAGAN's plan for full employment is nearly complete. As of today, nearly everyone in his family is working. Statistics also show that not a single millionaire is looking for work.

Real Estate

- The real estate agent told the prospective buyer, "Sure we have some $25,000 homes, but it will cost you $100,000."

Real Kibitzer

- The unmarried half of Siamese twins.

Recession

- The latest statistics tell us that more than five million Americans are idle. I'm sorry to report that most of them work for the government.

Reincarnation

- My neighbor says the possibility of reincarnation has him troubled. He's worried that if he comes back as a dog, his wife is sure to return as a flea.
- I definitely believe in reincarnation. Did you ever notice how many dead people come to life every day at five in the afternoon?

Relations

- Every month I go to Pittsburgh because I have relations there. Unfortunately, my wife just found out with whom.

Relatives

- Go to friends for advice, to women for sympathy, to strangers for charity, and to relatives for nothing.

Religion

- "Remember," the preacher was lecturing the group of modern young girls, "to resist temptation when it comes." One girl sighed, "I'd like to—but I'm afraid it may never come again."
- Las Vegas is the most religious city in the world. At any hour you can walk into a casino and hear someone say, "Oh, my God!"

Remarriage

- Nature's way of giving man a fresh start and a new leash on life.

Restaurant

- The food was so bad, when I asked for a doggy bag I was arrested for attempted cruelty to animals.
- A diner at Lindy's told his frantic waiter, "You know, I first came into this place in 1938." The waiter said, "I only got two hands. I'll get to your table in a minute."
- When a girl first marries, a man should never expect the first few meals to be very good. It takes time to find the right restaurants.

Retirement

- The lady of the house describes retirement as "twice as much husband on half as much income."

Rich

- He's so rich he's got money to burn. Why not? It's cheaper than gas.
- He's so rich he just had his gums capped.

Rock Music

- Comic HENRY HOLDEN asks, "Did you notice that all the rock fans these days are wearing ear phones? Personally, I prefer ear plugs."
- "If you like rock music," says JOE DOYLE, "you can't get enough rock; if you don't, you can't get enough rocks."

Romance

- At twenty-one you believe in long engagements. At forty-one you don't even believe in long introductions.
- The best way to prove girls are dynamite is to try to drop one.
- BURT REYNOLDS says, "I prefer a girl who's sexy, not brainy. When I feel intellectual I can always go to the public library."

- She was telling her friend, "Not only did the wise guy run out of gas—he had a trailer with him!"
- "I'm sure you'll like Charlie," she said to her father. "He's a very nice boy." Pop asked, "Does he have any money?" She asked, "Oh, you men are all alike. Charlie asked the same thing about you."
- STEVEN KESSLER said it: "There are two times in life a woman is looking for the right man. When she's single and later on when she's got an unmarried daughter."
- From the sexy mouth of JOE NAMATH: "They say a miss is as good as a mile, but I'm not so sure. After all, you can have a lot of fun with a miss, but what are you going to do with a mile?"
- BURT REYNOLDS doesn't give a second thought to women. His first thought covers everything.
- ZSA ZSA explains, "There's really nothing wrong with a woman welcoming all men's advances, darling, as long as they are in cash."

Rural Areas

- Those backward places that use a substance called money rather than credit cards.

Salesman

- An Arab sheik returned home from a vacation in the United States. A fellow sheik asked him, "What impressed you most about the Americans?" "Their salesmen," he replied, strapping on his skis.

Sanitation Department

- I saw this sign on a N.Y.C. garbage truck: "If you are not satisfied with our methods—you will receive double your garbage back."

Santa Claus

- When I was a kid I saw mommy kissing Santa Claus in seven different department stores.

Savings

- Remember when you saved up for your old age instead of for April 15?

Savoir Faire

- Three men were discussing savoir faire. One said, "If I go home and find my wife kissing another man and say, 'Excuse me,' that is savoir faire." The second said, "Not quite. If I come home and find my wife kissing another man and say, 'Excuse me—please continue,' that's savoir faire." The third said, "If I come home and find my wife kissing another man and I say 'Excuse me—please continue,' and he can continue, that's savoir fair."

Science

- One humiliating thing about science is that it is gradually filling our homes with appliances that are smarter than we are.

Secretary

- The executive said to his departing secretary, "In a way I'll be sorry to lose you. You've been like a daughter to me—insolent, surly, and unappreciative."
- The office manager said to the new secretary, "Fantastic, you've been with us only two weeks and you're already three weeks behind in your work." She screamed, "I'm sick and tired of your criticizing my work! I resign, do you hear? R-E-S-I-N-E!"
- Both partners were having a go at their secretary and both were shocked to learn that the young lady was pregnant. Each tried to blame the other. Finally, one of the partners went on a trip and while he was away the secretary was confined. Soon after, the traveler received a telegram from his partner: "Sally gave birth to twins—mine died."
- "Someday," the secretary complained about her boss, "I'm going to let the old fool catch me—just to see what he'd do."
- One big executive told me, "I don't fool with secretaries. I have one motto: "If at first I don't succeed—I fire her."

Senior Citizens

- Senior citizens still have their fun, thanks to that new wonder drug: prune juice.

Sex

- JOHN BARRYMORE said it and it still holds good today: "The thing that takes up the least amount of time and causes the most amount of trouble is sex."
- The man said, "I wouldn't call sex such a driving force. Personally, I prefer it when I'm parked somewhere."
- DR. JOYCE BROTHERS' prescription for a happy love life: "No matter how lovesick a girl may be, she shouldn't necessarily take the first pill that comes along."
- There are a lot of things I don't understand, like Doctor Reuben's book, *Everything You Wanted to Know About Sex*. He left out the most important part—where to get it.
- Personally, I don't think sex is that important. I much prefer a musical concert. But lately I've begun to notice that if I don't get to a concert for a year and a half, I don't miss it.
- A guy can tell when he's reached the dangerous age. That's when he starts trying to prove that he's just as good as he never was.
- BURT REYNOLDS says, "My problem is that girls are always running through my mind. Considering my thoughts, they wouldn't dare walk. . . . I don't mind sex and violence in the movies, but not while the picture is on.
- WOODY ALLEN explains, "I saw a picture that reminded me of my sex life. It was called *Coma*."
- The doc asked the salesman how active his love life was. He said, "Every Monday, Tuesday, Wednesday, and Friday regularly." Doc said, "Maybe that's your problem. I suggest you cut out Fridays." The salesman said, "I can't doc. That's the only night of the week I'm home."
- The speaker was introduced as "an expert on sex." He got up and said, "It gives me great pleasure," and he sat down.
- My neighbor says he's a great lover: "Last night with my wife I gave the performance of my life—I almost woke her up."

- No one wants you for your mind—but for what you don't mind.
- Sex is like business. When it's good it's wonderful, and when its bad, it's still pretty good.

Sex Education

- It's silly to teach kids sex education in school. Like everything else, they'll just forget it when they grow up.

Sexual Compatability

- After 30 years of married life, last week my neighbor and his wife reached total sexual compatability. They both had a headache.

Signs

- Signs in bar: "If you drink to forget, please pay in advance." "If you must drive your husband to drink—drive him here."
- Sign at fire hydrant: "Park now—pay later."
- Sign at farm: "Eggs laid while you wait."

Skiers

- Good skiers are made of one mold—plaster of paris.

Skiing

- I went to one ski resort that had three slopes: beginners', intermediates', and call-an-ambulance.
- The Nevele in the Catskills has a Twiggy ski slope and a Dolly Parton ski slope. The Dolly Parton naturally has lots of curves.

Small Town

- This town is so small the telephone directory only lists first names.
- This town is so small, their telephone directory has one yellow page.
- This town is so small, the female impersonator is a woman.

Smoking

- There's a filling station that displays a big sign reading, "No smoking: Your life may not be worth much, but gasoline is!"
- People who give up smoking have the same problem as the newcomer in the nudist camp—they don't know what to do with their hands.

Snob

- A snob is a person who only wants to know the people who don't want to know him.

Social Security

- The problem of retiring at sixty-five is that the annual income you once set as your goal is now below poverty level.
- RONALD REAGAN is the first President to collect social security before his first paycheck.

Socialism and Capitalism

- With socialism, if you have two cars you give one to your neighbor. With capitalism, if you have two cars you sell one and buy a bull.

Socialized Medicine

- Co-ed recovery rooms.

Society

- This society playboy (in a small town he'd be known as the town drunk—the only thing he did for a living is read his father's will) looked down at Mr. Cohen and sneered, "One of my ancestors signed the Declaration of Independence." "So?" Mr. Cohen answered. "One of mine signed the Ten Commandments."

Specialized Medicine

- Medicine has become so specialized nowadays that when my head cold moved down to my chest, I had to change doctors.

Spender
- My wife has a black belt in shopping.

Spinster
- Nature's frozen asset.
- A woman who spends her life in solitary refinement.

Sports
- I can understand why so many people love professional sports these days. After all, what else gives you a chance to boo a bunch of millionaires to their faces.

Sports for Women
- Girls who are good sports go out more than anybody.

Statesman
- A politician who never got caught.
- A statesman is a man who thinks he belongs to the state; a politician is a man who thinks the state belongs to him.

Stock Market
- With the present market conditions, I'm the first to admit that I'm neither a bull nor a bear—I'm chicken.
- This is a country of faith. On the installment plan you can buy what you can't afford—in the stock market, you can sell what you don't own.
- A stock market investor is someone who is alert, informed, attuned to the economic heartbeat of America—and cries a lot.

Stockbroker
- A stockbroker is always ready to back his judgment with your last dollar

David Stockman
- To the tune of "Jingle Bells":

Budget cuts, budget cuts,
Slashing all the way;
Everything must be reduced—
Except, of course, my pay.

Strip Joint

- Salesmen who come to Broadway spend their lonely nights at a club that offers entertainment. If the girls' clothes don't drop off, the attendance does.

Stuffy

- He's the kind who would go to a porno movie and complain about the background music.

Suburbs

- By the time you finish paying for your home in the suburbs, they are no longer suburbs.
- Freddie bought an $8,000 house for $94,000. He says, "Congratulate me. In only twelve years my wife and I have just finished paying off the first $100 on the principal of our mortgage."

Success

- Success is relative. The more success, the more relatives.
- If at first you succeed, you're probably in your father's business.
- A successful man is one who earns more than his wife can spend; a successful woman is one who finds such a man.
- Success is the good fortune compounded of ambition, hard work, and marriage to the boss's daughter.

Summer Vacation

- Summertime is the greatest for those nice, long weekend motor trips. One day driving and two days folding the road maps.

Superstition

- I'm not the superstitious type. I figure before you put too much faith in a rabbit's foot, for instance, remember it didn't do much for the rabbit.

Supreme Being

- My neighbor says, "I speak from experience. I *know* there's a supreme being—*my wife.*"

Sympathy

- What you give a friend or relative when you don't want to lend him money.

Tax Collectors

- Tax collectors and psychiatrists are giving out the same advice—it's not good for a man to keep too much to himself.

Tax Shelter

- My neighbor says he has a foolproof tax shelter—poverty.

Taxes

- I dreamed that I saw a beautiful rainbow and started walking in search of the end of it. And when I came to the end of the rainbow, there really was a pot of gold there! And standing right next to the pot of gold was an IRS agent!
- I feel like writing a letter to the income tax bureau and telling them I can no longer afford their service.
- After filing my income tax returns for this year, the only thing I expect to get back from the IRS is an audit.
- My revenue agent told me, "Listen, we sympathize with your problems, but the thing is, they won't fit in a computer."
- One guy wrote the tax boys, "If this is a free country, how come I can't afford it?"
- A taxpayer called the IRS to ask if he could take a certain deduction on his income tax. The answer was, "No!" followed by, "This is a recorded announcement."

- My neighbor was furious because the tax boys ruled that a baby born in January is not deductible in last year's income. He hollered, "I can't understand it. It was last year's business."
- I hear talk about lowering taxes. I hope they lower them down enough so we can pay them.
- They get you coming and going. If you win something, it's minus taxes; if you buy something it's plus taxes.
- Historians are still trying to convince us that the United States was founded to avoid taxation.
- The trouble with tax loopholes is that there isn't enough for everybody.
- I wouldn't mind the government's living beyond it's income if it wasn't also living beyond mine.
- Now I hear the IRS is selling gift certificates.
- An IRS man is writing a book called, *How We Made $1.8 Million Off the Fellow Who Wrote a Book About Making $2 Million in the Stock Market.*
- In the words of the kindly old income tax collector, "It is better to give then to receive—and it's safer too!"
- Sign in the window of H & R Schlock, tax experts: "Let us prepare your taxes and save you time. Like five to ten years."

Taxpayer

- The biggest job Congress has is how to get the money from the taxpayer without disturbing the votes.

Teenager

- A teenager is an adolescent who is constantly irked by her disobedient parents.
- Today's teens don't think they're having a good time unless they're doing something their parents can't afford.
- I was held up the other night by a teenage thug who told me, "Gimme all your money—and make it snappy, I gotta be home by ten."
- No wonder today's teenager is confused. Half the adults are telling him to find himself and the other half are telling him to get lost.

Telephone

- All the world loves a lover—except when you're waiting to use the telephone.
- ZSA ZSA claims, "America's best buy is still a 10-cent call to the right man."

Television

- All stations now have TV archaeologists. They're the guys who dig up the movies for the late show.
- You think TV is bad now? Go to the movies and see what it's going to be like in ten years.
- The greatest spectacle of the year was my TV repairman's bill.
- TV has made dull conversationalists of us all. It even has people to talk about the weather for us.
- Most people enjoy television because it takes them away from the frustrations of real life. Me, I enjoy real life because it takes me away from television.
- BETTE DAVIS explains, "Television is a completely self-contained medium. It not only gives you a headache, but it sells you a cure for it, too."

The Ten Commandments

- The reason why the Ten Commandments are short and clear is that they were handed down direct—not through several committees.

Texas

- This gorgeous redhead was introduced to this Texas millionaire and asked, "How much did you say your name is?"
- I know a Texan so rich he owns an unlisted telephone company.
- I know a Texan who is so rich that he doesn't even bother to buy air-conditioned cars. He just keeps a couple of cold ones in his freezer.
- I know a man from Texas who is so lazy that he gave his wife an oil well for her birthday, just so he wouldn't have to wrap any presents.

- I know a Texan who was so excited before his first child was born that when his wife developed a craving for mints, he tried to buy her Fort Knox.

Thrifty

- My wife is very thrifty. She didn't want to buy an Easter bonnet because she'd only wear it once—so she bought a mink coat suitable for all occasions.

Toys

- I saw one toy in a department store marked, "X-mas special $25." I asked, "What was it *before* Christmas?" The salesman said, "$5.95."

Traffic

- America is a nation that adds every year a hundred new cars for every new parking space.
- 'Tis the season to complain about the traffic. Well, don't complain. If there were fewer cars on the road, it would be even harder to find a parking place.
- There is only one way to solve the traffic problem. Keep all the cars that are not paid for off the streets.
- Year by year it takes less time to fly around the world—and more and more time to drive to work.
- Traffic is getting worse. This morning on the Long Island Expressway you had to get on a waiting list. Then you go back home and when there's an opening they call you.
- I was lucky on my trip this summer. They had the highway open while the detour was being fixed.

Travel

- A road map tells you everything you need to know—except how to fold it up again.
- After seeing those backwoods, broken-down counties, it's good to be back home living in New York and seeing those broken-down streets.

- She signed up for one of those economy cruises. She stays home and the company sends her picture postcards to mail.
- If you didn't go on a vacation this year, you can get the feel of one by tipping every third person you see.
- Did you ever notice that a bus goes twice as fast when you're chasing it as it does when you're on it?
- When you start to look like your passport picture—you know you need a vacation.
- "Good news! I've saved enough money for us to go to Europe," she said excitedly. "Wonderful," her husband said, "When do we leave?" She explained, "As soon as I've saved enough for us to come back."
- GEORGE BURNS says, "Flying is more fun these days. At my age the biggest kick I get is being frisked at airports. . . . On my last trip to Europe Sophia Loren was there and they frisked her for two hours—and she was seeing someone off."

Ugly

- He took his kid to the zoo and the man at the gate thanked him for returning the kid.

Unemployment

- PRESIDENT REAGAN says, "I don't care what anybody says, there's just no chance of really ever getting rid of unemployment. Once the unemployment experts solve unemployment, *they'll* be unemployed!"
- There's one good thing about unemployment. When you get up in the morning you're already there.

Unions

- Many workers in America are already on a three-day week. They just take five days to get through it.

Unlucky

- The waiter was complaining, "I'm so unlucky that if it rained soup, everybody would have a spoon and I'd be left with a fork."

Used Cars

- My car is getting old. My mechanic said, "Your headlights have cataracts."
- RIP TAYLOR warns, "Never buy a car that's being sold at the bottom of a ravine."
- I drive an '82. That's not the year—that's the resale value."

USSR

- ANTHONY PERAINO reports: YURI ANDROPOV fancied himself a world traveler. One Soviet diplomat asked him what he thought of New York. Yuri replied, "New York is a nice place to visit, but I wouldn't want to invade there."

Vacation

- In Tibet, I met a man who was 150 years old. He looked like 20—singing, happy, joyful. I asked how he keeps his youth. He said, "Pills, my boy, pills." I asked, "Pills? How many do you take a day?" He said, "I don't take them, I sell them."
- They were such a nice couple. They went on a cruise to celebrate their twenty-fifth wedding anniversary. Everything was just perfect. "Gee," the man said to his wife, "this could be such a romantic night if we weren't stuck with each other."
- "We're saving a fortune on our trip to Hawaii this year," LEE GUBER told me, "We're not going."
- My friend took his wife and mother-in-law with him on a safari in Africa, and one day his mother-in-law disappeared. They found her behind a ledge and this huge lion was standing over her. His wife cried, "What should we do?" He said, "Nothing. That lion got himself into that mess, now let him get out of it."
- JERRY WHITE says, "This year I'm going to save money by just getting hijacked somewhere and staying there."
- Taking a vacation has only one problem. You can turn off the gas, you can turn off the electricity, but you can't turn off the rent.

Valentine's Day

- The lady next door got this lovely Valentine: "You're the best little wife a guy ever had, even if your husband doesn't think so."
- Holding the gorgeous blonde in his arms, he drooled, "I love you, dear, as no man has ever loved you before." She said, "Funny, I can't tell the difference."
- Their car stopped on the edge of a secluded road. The young man said to his date, "It's Valentine's Day. If I try to make love to you, will you yell for help?" She cooed, "Only if you really need it."
- He said, "I must insist on knowing one thing. Am I the first man to sleep with you?" She said, "You will be darling, if you doze off."

Vanity

- I know a woman so vain, she even lies about her dog's age.

Vice President

- People are inclined to underestimate the importance of the VP. Just remember, he presides over the Senate, is the President's rep all over the world, and during Cabinet meetings, he's the one who goes out for coffee.

Violence

- On TV last night one program had seven murders, three robberies, and one attempted rape—and that was on sermonette.

Virgin

- She says she's a virgin—but she's not a fanatic about it.

Virtue and Vice

- The difference between virtue and vice is that the first is usually learned at mother's knee, while the latter is learned at some other joint.

Voluptuous

- A woman who has curves in places where some girls don't even have places!

Voting

- My neighbor says, "Why should I vote? All the candidates have promised me everything I ever wanted."

Wall Street

- Investment clubs are the big thing on Wall Street today. They're a way to lose money by parliamentary procedure.
- Wall Street has three kinds of investors: bulls, bears and asses.

George Washington

- One sure thing we know about George, he wasn't a sailor. Anybody who stands up in a boat, can't be a sailor. . . . But he was the greatest. He lacked only one big accomplishment—an interview with Barbara Walters.

Wealth

- Only the rich can be eccentric. The poor have to be satisfied with just being nuts.

Wedding

- PUDGY took a poll and found out that most young couples today hold off a wedding ceremony till they can afford a baby-sitter.
- A ceremony at which a woman takes a man for what he is or what he has.

White House

- "I don't care what anybody says," notes BOB HOPE, "REAGAN is the nicest tourist we ever had in the White House—and Nancy sets a nice table. If he really wants to balance the budget, he can rent out his rooms."

- The White House has just been added to the map of movie stars' homes.
- NANCY REAGAN spent $300,000 to fix up the White House—just to remove the grit stains.

Wife

- A man should never judge his wife too harshly for her weaknesses. If she didn't have them, chances are she wouldn't have married him.
- A wife is a woman who will stick by you in all the trouble you wouldn't have gotten into if you hadn't married her in the first place.

Wills

- The wife asked the lawyers, "You mean I could have a mink coat, a new car, and a trip around the world—and all he has to do is pass away?"
- HAROLD GARY told me he is willing his body to science and, "while I'm alive, to RAQUEL WELCH."
- Many a girl is looking for an older man with a strong will—made out to her.

Windfall Profits

- When your dime comes back at the pay phone.

Wingo

- The man was told he won $50,000 in WINGO. He was asked, "What's the first thing you're going to do?" He said, "Tell my relatives it wasn't me!"

Winters

- LONI ANDERSON says, "I really know how to survive severe winter weather. I take vitamin C. I take it all the way to Acapulco and stay there."

Wolf

- He's got a good head on his shoulders—but it's a different one every night.

Women

- It's a woman's world. When a man is born, the first question is, "How's the mother." When he marries, it's, "What a lovely bride," and when he dies, the question is, "How much did he leave her?"
- Women have an advantage. Seems to me if they can't get what they want by being smart, they get it by being dumb.

Women Drivers

- BERNIE ALLEN told me, "My wife took my new car and hit a tree. She said it wasn't her fault: 'I blew the horn.'"
- Life is a paradox. Many a woman who can easily thread a needle has trouble getting a car into a garage.
- MORTY GUNTY says, "My poor wife failed her driving test for one lousy mistake. She ran over the guy giving her the test."

Women's Lib

- When you meet someone who loves to cook and do housework, don't hesitate—marry him.
- An actor pal told me he is doing all he can to help the women's liberation movement. "The first thing I did was divorce my wife."
- GEORGE BURNS says, "My mother with all her kids wouldn't have understood this women's lib stuff about getting out of the kitchen. What my mother wanted was to get *into* the kitchen. What she wanted *out* of was the bedroom."
- Too many girls get married before they can adequately support a husband.
- The husband lectured his wife, "Stick to your washing, ironing, scrubbing, and cooking. No wife of mine is going to work."
- ANGIE DICKENSON says, "When the wife wears the pants—some other woman wears the fur coat."

Work

- People are still willing to do an honest day's work—only they want a week's pay for it.

World News

- Did you know that in China there are more children born every minute than in India, and in India there are more children born than in Turkey? Which proves, more people talk turkey in India than in Turkey.

Wrinkles

- Wrinkles are hereditary. Parents get them from their children.

Youth

- A girl can learn a lot on her mother's knee. But she forgets it all once she switches to a man's lap.
- MYRNA LOY said it, "There's nothing wrong with our young people today that becoming a parent and taxpayer won't cure."

Zsa Zsa Gabor

- "Diamonds are a girl's best friend and dogs are man's best friend. Now you know which sex has more sense."